Fishing up the Moon

Norfolk Seafood Cookery

The Year of a
Norfolk Longshoreman

described
by

David Stannard

and
illustrated
by

George Smith

The Larks Press

Published by the Larks Press
Ordnance Farmhouse
Guist Bottom, Dereham, Norfolk NR20 5PF
01328 829207
Larks.Press@btinternet.com

Printed by the Lanceni Press
Garrood Drive, Fakenham

June 2005

For Rosamond

Also by David Stannard
Broader Norfolk – a Quizzionary of Norfolk Dialect

British Library Cataloguing–in–Publication Data
A catalogue record for this book is available from the British Library

ISBN 1 904006 26 4

FOREWORD

This book is about sea-fish and sea fishing: how to catch sea-fish and shell fish, how to prepare these products of the sea for the kitchen, and then how to combine these basic ingredients to produce dishes for the table which will delight the palate and bring out the best that the waters of the North Sea can offer.

This certainly isn't a book about angling; you will not find here any useful hints on how to capture fish in order to play with them for sport then return them, alive but exhausted to the water. Neither does the art of fly fishing for salmon and trout merit any attention in this work, for the object of this sport appears to be to make it as difficult as possible to make a catch using artificial lures.

You will find described here the techniques used to secure a wide variety of fish for the table; it is to be hoped that modern science will allow the exploitation of these marine species to continue to be a viable and fruitful area of human endeavour.

This work is intended to celebrate the ingenuity and skill of generations of men and women, who have brought fish from the sea to the table for the delight and nourishment of the diner. The reader can choose to opt out of any stage of this process. If that means just enjoying the final products of the labours of others, then at least the diner will have the satisfaction of appreciating just how the dish was brought to the table, and the enjoyment will be enhanced by that knowledge.

The book is broadly split into four sections, reflecting the seasons of the sea. In a supermarket-dominated world, which insists on offering identical produce on every single week of the year, there is little room for the the simple pleasure of anticipation which the seasons provide or for the sense of fulfilment derived from a memorable dish enjoyed in season.

Eccles-on-Sea 2005

CONTENTS

INTRODUCTION

With well over fifty miles of coastline bordering the county we should not be surprised that the residents of Norfolk have gained considerable experience in catching the bounty of the North Sea, and also in turning this bounty into any number of interesting and tasty dishes. Indeed, these skills have served Norfolk well, for in combination with the harvest of the land the rich pickings from the sea have provided the basis of the county's economy since time immemorial. It is no accident that some of the country's largest food processors are located in Norfolk, as indeed is the United Kingdom's leading food research institute. And while we may only gain moderate satisfaction from knowing that the fish finger was invented in Great Yarmouth, even this humble fare must take its place with pride alongside the kipper and bloater by which that town gained culinary fame and fortune.

Go north from Great Yarmouth and you will find the chalky shores off Cromer and Sheringham that have sustained a commercial crab and lobster fishery for well over 150 years, while to the west the flat, wide beaches of Wells, Holkham and Brancaster yield a wide variety of sessile shellfish including cockles, mussels and oysters. The shallow waters of the Wash, with its many sandbanks, are home to both prawns and brown shrimps, which are exploited by any number of small shrimpers, plying their trade from the port of King's Lynn. In between these centres of commercial fishery, small boats launched from the beaches seek out the bounty of the sea in much the same way as they have done since human beings first learned to build boats and braid nets.

In recent times the surge of interest in fine foods has caused numerous eating houses across East Anglia to spring up to capitalise on the availability of fresh foodstuffs, with fish and shellfish being high on the list of priorities for their menus. So it is that the rest of the world is discovering, perhaps re-discovering, two things that Norfolk people have known for centuries, that truly excellent food can only come from really fresh ingredients, and that these can best be obtained by those living closest to their source.

This book takes a seasonal look at the wide variety of fish and shellfish that our Norfolk shores can provide. It reveals some of the secrets that go into processing these creatures to make them palatable, and then suggests ways to combine the products into dishes of incomparable delight. Finally, in true Norfolk style, it encourages economy by suggesting ways of turning even the leftovers into yet more tasty dishes, or preserving them for leaner days to come.

But first, as every longshoreman knows, you have to catch your fish, and to catch them successfully you must know something of their habits, for as the seasons change, so do the species that come to our shores. Many fish species are temporary visitors, following the dictates of sun, moon, tide and temperature in their need to reproduce. Many shellfish species live on our shores throughout the year, but are only fit for eating at certain times or only become active when the sea temperature rises. The clever longshoreman sets his pots, nets and lines in the right place at the right time to catch his prey, but even the cleverest fisherman will acknowledge that an essential element in securing a decent catch is a sizeable dollop of good luck!

Traditional Norfolk 'double-ender' fishing boats

CHAPTER ONE
SPRING

'...did yer have yer tea by daylight on Walentens?'
The Boy John Letters (February 22nd 1951)
Sidney Grapes

St Valentine's Eve (February 14th) is always a special day in Norfolk for two reasons aside from the romantic associations usually connected with this saint's feast day. The first reason is that this is the evening when Jack Valentine pays his surreptitious, and curiously unique, visits to Norfolk homes. If the occupants have been well-behaved boys and girls this mysterious benefactor (no one has ever actually seen him of course) leaves his calling card at the front door in the form of a loud knock and a gift-wrapped present. However, his mischievous nature also means that sometimes a knock is his only gift and no present is to be found on the doorstep!

The second reason is that on this day, for the first time in the year, Norfolk residents can expect to have their tea, around half past four in the afternoon, in daylight. This is something that undoubtedly tries the patience of the capricious Jack Valentine, and his young beneficiaries. So too, as the days lengthen, will the more measured patience of the seasoned Norfolk longshoreman be stirred to consider things to come.

By Valentine's day he will have checked over and repaired his pots, tows and dahns in anticipation of the coming crab and lobster season as these creature themselves come out of hibernation and start to feed after their winter fast. And as he scrapes the pot and spreads the final fragrant remnants of last season's crab paste over his buttered bread, his thoughts will also turn to all of those wonderful freshly boiled shellfish teas which await the fortunate crabber.

Crabs and Crabbers

Commercial fishermen set baited pots or nets well out to sea to catch edible (brown) crabs and lobsters. The first crab pot was introduced into north Norfolk from the North Shields area in the 1860s; before that time the fishermen had used flat, basket-shaped hooped nets to catch their quarry. These were baited and left for a time on the seabed and then steadily hauled to the surface; if they were lucky they would get two or three decent-sized specimens, but all too often the net would capsize and the catch would be lost. The four-hooped crab pot proved to be a revolutionary piece of technology which would allow the fishermen to set the baited traps, leave technology which would allow the fishermen to set the baited traps, leave them for a couple of tides and return the next day in the certain knowledge that any mature crustacean that had been caught would not have escaped. The trap relies on the fact that edible crabs cannot swim; drop an edible into the water and it sinks like a stone to the bottom of the sea. When caught, the crabs can crawl all over the inside of their ingeniously contrived prison, but they cannot make that essential jump to return through the net tunnel (the 'crinny') by which they entered the pot. Plaice 'frames', the waste left when the fillets have been removed, were traditionally used as bait, and fishermen would ring the changes with whole herring or mackerel as the fancy took them; these days the bait is usually kept in the freezer ready for use.

Crabbers soon developed the potting method into a commercial operation by joining together a dozen or more pots with ropes ('tows') to form a 'shank' of pots. The last pot at either end of the shank is connected by a further tow to an anchor, which fixes the long line of pots to the seabed. A longer tow attached to the fluke of each anchor terminates in a floating buoy, locally called a 'dahn'; these carry distinctive flags to identify which shank of pots belongs to whom. Potting proved to be so successful in the 1860s that within a decade serious concern was expressed for the future of the fishery due to over-fishing. The Government despatched a naturalist, Francis Buckland, to Cromer to investigate the situation, and his subsequent report made recommendations to regulate the size of crabs and lobsters that could legally be landed. These were quickly introduced as local byelaws, and with the help of other restrictions, intended to preserve stocks, the situation was saved. In particular, fishermen were not allowed to land 'berried' lobsters, i.e. ones that were carrying eggs. Such restrictions, with minor modifications, still prevail in Norfolk today and the sustainability of the fishery is being properly maintained.

Setting the crab-pots

The traditional craft used for the fishery were wooden 'double-ender' crab boats with a pointed bow and stern, a design some claim to be based on the Saxon and Viking longboats that invaded the Norfolk coast in the Dark Ages. Initially powered by oars and sail, the boat was adapted to facilitate launching, and more importantly landing, in this area where even the slightest north winds quickly pick up the sea, producing fearsome breakers on the flat sand and shingle beaches. In such conditions any boat with a flat, broad transom would be liable to capsize, putting lives at risk; the pointed stern of a double-ender made it easier to avoid such tragedy.

Setting shanks of crabs pots is hard physical work, undertaken when the tide is starting to run to ensure the anchors get a good grip on the seabed; retrieving them is even harder. Using muscle power alone, this is only possible during the ten to fifteen minutes of slack water which occurs twice a day when the tide changes direction; at other times the strength of the tidal current is enormous and soon saps the energy of even the strongest fisherman. Thus the timing of the operation is dictated partly by the prevailing weather, but even more by the state of the tide, and with a family to feed the longshore crabber is often forced to make hard judgements when bad weather threatens.

Inevitably risks were taken in treacherous waters (go due north from Cromer and there's nothing but open sea until you reach the polar ice cap) and accidents and tragedies frequently occurred. But the invention in the 1960s of the compact, hydraulically operated 'pot puller' changed all that. These devices, powered by the inboard diesel engines, which in the previous decade had become the norm for local crab boats, gave greater flexibility in venturing offshore, as well as making the job physically much easier. Nowadays, the use of modern flat-bottomed fibreglass skiffs, powered by high horsepower engines, allows the crabbers to get offshore quickly and check large numbers of pots in half the time taken by the traditional double-ender crab boats. This also means that the timing of the operation can now be geared more to market needs rather than tidal influences, for every crabber has to be a good businessman as well as a clever fisherman in order to make a reasonable living from such a perishable product. But no matter how powerful the boat, or how efficient the fishing gear, there will always be times when it will prove impossible to launch or land safely on the Norfolk coast. Even though the sun may be shining on land, the wind and sea conditions will keep the frustrated crabber kicking his heels in the fishing shed, and the innocent holidaymaker wondering why there are no crabs for sale that day.

Shore Crabbing

Commercial crabbers hunt their quarry well offshore, but what of the shore hunters, can they find crabs on the beaches of Norfolk? Well the answer is yes, but only if they look in the right places. There are five common species of crab that inhabit our shores; edible (brown) crabs *(Cancer paguras)*, hermit crabs *(Eupagurus bernhardus)*, shore crabs *(Carcinus maenas)*, swimming crabs *(Porcellana platycheles)*, known locally as kittywitches, and velvet crabs *(Portunus puber)*. Examples of the last three are often found in shrimp nets, the porcelain-coloured swimming crab is distinguished from the greenish, browny-red shore crabs by the two red-tinted paddle-shaped claws that allow this crab to swim, while the velvet crab, also a swimmer, is covered with a coat of fine hairs the colour and texture of plush brown suede. Hermit crabs are the ones that inhabit old whelk shells. Whilst all these crabs are indeed edible (see Lobster Bisque p. 00) the most plentiful meat is found in the edible crab and this is the only crab species that is fished commercially in Norfolk, especially off Cromer and Sheringham where the chalk of the seabed provides ideal hidey holes for them to thrive.

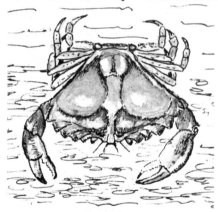

Shore Crab

However, for the Norfolk shore fisherman the flat northern beaches around Holme and Brancaster can provide specimens of edible crabs, for they may be found inhabiting holes in the clay and peat beds exposed on the beach at low tides. Eager hunters armed with short hooked sticks can, with skill, hoik out an edible from its lair; cod fishermen use a similar technique in search of soft-shelled shore crabs, an irresistible lure to their quarry when put on the hook. The reason the crab is soft-shelled is that it will recently have moulted, and if the shore crabber spots the cast-off moult he can usually be sure that a soft-shell will be lurking in a hidey hole close by. When a female shore crab is about to moult she will often associate with a fully mature male crab who will wrap his pincers around the female in a protective embrace until she has finished moulting and her new shell has hardened. The couple, referred to by the old fishermen as a 'Man and Wife' or 'Rab and Bab', will then part and proceed on their way, unless of course they are discovered by a shore fisherman who will separate the female and put it in his bait can. Edible crabs also moult, but be warned, the crab fishery bye-laws still apply to the beach crabbers and they forbid the use of edible crabs as bait. Woe betide anyone who takes an edible crab for food which is less than 115mm (4½ inches) across the broadest part of the carapace!

Having caught your crab, the traditional method of calming it down before bagging it is to spit in its face, but simply folding your hands over the creature to encourage it to draw up its legs and pincers will usually have the desired effect, and shielding its eyes from the light for a few moments will also help. I have successfully

Hermit Crab

used this technique on everything from Louisianan crawfish to Welsh spider crabs, while a lobster can be calmed by firmly stroking its underside with the back of a knife. You can then stand the creature on its head with the claws forward as a triangular support, a neat party trick, but not really much use for anything else! No matter what method you choose to catch or calm your crabs or lobsters, in order to make them palatable you will need to make some basic preparations to clean and cook the creatures before removing the meat from their shells. Having secured the meat, you can then choose to eat it straight away, or combine it with other ingredients into the range of dishes described below.

The Basic Preparation of Crabs and Lobsters

If you are going to seek out edible crabs or lobsters *(Homarus vulgaris)* from sources other than the fishmonger's slab, you will need to know how to do the basic preparation that is usually undertaken by suppliers before the shellfish are offered for sale. Only the most expensive restaurants have a tank of live lobster swimming around for you to choose one for your dinner. Having made your choice, the chef will extract the appropriate specimen and take it back to the kitchen, (where perhaps it should have remained) to plunge it live into boiling water. If you flinch at the thought, please remember that stories about the animal screaming at such a painful death are highly exaggerated, and usually explained by the noise made when the air trapped under the carapace is expelled as steam.

At home in your kitchen you can use a far less dramatic way to cook shellfish; indeed if you tried the boiling plunge method with a Cromer crab all the legs and claws would instantly drop off, leaving a very odd-looking specimen for the table. To avoid this, having secured your crabs, don't cook them straight away but keep them for a few hours in tepid water to allow them to cleanse themselves ('to let 'em spit' is the traditional phrase). This also tends to relax the shellfish and make them less active, but take care that the animals are not allowed to expire during this process for cooking a dead crab or lobster will produce a highly undesirable, if not positively dangerous result. Having steeped the shellfish, proceed to take the live crab or lobster, and, using an old toothbrush, give it a good scrub under running water to remove all the mud that adheres to the hairy shells of these bottom-living creatures. Make sure you get at bits under the main claws, which you may wish to wrap with elastic bands to avoid getting nipped. (A large crab or lobster has enough hydraulic power in its claws to crush a finger bone; 'handle with care' is always the rule of the day.) Place the cleaned shellfish into a large pan containing about an inch (25mm) of cold water and three large tablespoons of salt (1½ ounces of salt to the pint). Put the lid on and bring the water slowly to the boil. The idea is to steam rather than boil the shellfish, so keep the lid tightly shut. When they are boiling keep them simmering for at least six minutes for a small crab, double that time for a large crab or lobster. Remove from the heat and give them another good scrub to remove the white scum that usually forms at the joints during cooking. (This is the natural glue that they exude when the shell gets broken in a fight.) Allow them to cool and refrigerate ready for dressing. The RSPCA recommend this way as being painless to the shellfish and relies on the fact that the animals get progressively dopier as the water heats up and will expire when it gets to 80°C; a further school of thought recommends placing live lobsters in the freezer for an hour to make them really dopey as a prelude to placing in the pan.

An alternative method for lobster is to kill the animal just prior to placing it in fiercely boiling water, a method recommended by those who claim that the application of high heat instantly seals the meat of the lobster in the same way as a piece of steak is seared in a frying pan, thus ensuring that all the juices, and flavour are retained. Place the lobster on a stout board and hammer the blunt side of a cleaver or heavy knife down between the carapace and the tail. It will be killed instantly. I know of no way to kill an edible crab effectively, and any number of gory stories come from those who have tried. Stick to gentle boiling is my best recommendation. I am also a little sceptical about the boiling water theory for lobsters; I suspect that the thick carapace of a lobster acts as a perfectly good insulator, effectively preventing the sealing effect described. However there is one final method that does require you to kill the animal first and that is barbecuing. The convenient thing about barbecuing or grilling a lobster is that it comes with its own naturally built-in cooking pot!

12

Dressing Edible (Brown) Crabs

Professional crab dressers use a specially prepared instrument made from an old table knife to dress (or 'pick') a crab. To extract the meat from the various parts of the creature the blade of the knife is ground down to form a narrow quarter inch (5mm) wide blade about two inches (5cm) long with a rounded tip. Alternatively you can use a small vegetable knife with a long point, or buy a specially made shellfish pick from a good kitchen shop. You will also need a bowl for the meat (two bowls if you want to keep brown and white meat separate) and a chopping board or thick wad of paper on which to work. Start by prising open the crab, exposing the internal shell, the 'crown' or 'shekel', to which are attached the legs. This contains white meat; the brown meat is found inside the separated shell, which in Norfolk is variously known as the 'cart' or the 'boat'. Deal with this first. You will need to remove the stomach sac by turning the cart the right way up and pushing firmly with your thumb on the bit of shell between the crab's eyes. Doing so will snap off this part of the shell, and by a bit of gentle teasing the attached stomach sac, which looks like a small plastic bag, can be separated from the brown meat. Discard this sac and also the thin, transparent membrane that separates the brown meat from the shell. On the underside of the cart you will find a curved line in the shell, which naturally separates when the crab is ready to moult. Break the cart along this line to make it easier to remove the brown meat; make sure that none of the grey, tapered gills, attached to the brown meat, end up in your bowl.

Now turn your attention to the shekel, which provides protection for the internal organs and support for the legs and claws. Remove the rest of the grey gills, which surround the 'crown' of the shekel; these are called 'dead men's fingers' for obvious reasons. Peculiarly in Norfolk they are called 'deaf ears' which may relate to a fancied similarity to the long pointed ears of a donkey. The gills have a reputation for being poisonous which is not really true; it is simply that they may contain micro-organisms that the crab has filtered out from the seawater. It makes sense to avoid eating these organisms; if the crab won't eat them then neither should you. Using your knife, lever up and pull off the tail parts. If they are very wide you have a female 'hen' crab (in Norfolk dialect 'a broadster' or 'broad-apron crab'), if narrow then you have a male or 'jack' crab, which tends to have bigger claws than the females. Make sure that no black thread of the gut, which you will find under the tail, remains to spoil your tea.

If you wish, you can put the two halves back together and serve the crab on a bed of salad, providing a small pick and pair of nutcrackers for your guests to remove the meat themselves. The *Booke of Kervinge (1508)* lists some thirty terms to be applied to the carving of various fish and fowls, and

Dressing a Crab

Twisting off the legs

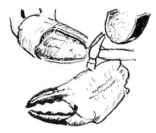

Cracking the claws

Extracting meat from the legs

Pulling the body from the shell

Removing intestines

Scraping out the brown meat

Trimming the shell

Dressed crab ready for serving

14

according to its author, Wynkyn de Worde, one should 'tame' a crab and 'barb' a lobster, but these days it is more usual to 'pick' both of these creatures. 'Picking', and all that the word implies in terms of taking your time over relishing tasty morsels, is an essential part of an *Assiette de Mer*. (See the recipe below for how to prepare a Norfolk version of this classic French dish.) This is also the point at which you can freeze your crabs, also described below. To dress the crab fully, remove and retain all the legs and claws, but discard the curved and fringed mouthparts.

You should now be ready to extract the meat from the shekel. This complex arched structure contains a lot of white meat, but in getting to it be careful that you don't include bits of the white shell in your bowl. Insert the point of your knife into each of the holes in the shekel where the legs were joined to the body. There are large chunks of meat at the base of each leg that, with a dextrous twist of the blade, can easily be removed. If necessary cut through the shekel horizontally to get at any remaining shreds of white meat; avoid the temptation to divide the shekel vertically. Finally, using the back of the knife or a pair of nutcrackers, crack the large claws and legs and extract the rest of the white meat. Some people prefer to keep the brown and white meat separate; others mash it all together to form an aromatic light brown pâté. A traditional method of presentation is to put the two sorts of meat back into a scrubbed-out cart with decorative lines of chopped boiled egg and parsley separating the brown and white meat. The choice is yours.

Preparing Velvet Crabs

Velvet or fiddler crabs (*Portunus puber*) are largely ignored as food in this country but go to France and you will find boxes of these creatures on the fishmonger's shelves. Smaller and more delicate than edible crabs (the legal minimum size limit is 65mm or about 2½ inches) there is not so much meat in them, but what there is has a sweeter, nuttier flavour than brown edible crabs. It is this delicate flavour which is highly prized by the French, who invariably serve them in an *Assiette de Mer* comprising a wide range of boiled shellfish all served on a bed of ice and seaweed. Velvet crabs are not easily obtainable from fishmongers but the Norfolk coast crabbers catch them in pots and will save some for you if you

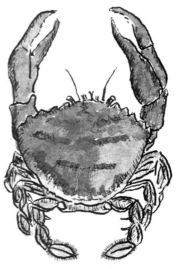

Velvet Crab

15

ask. Since velvets seem to favour rocky coastlines you will find them if you try shrimping around one of the Sea Palling reefs at low water. To cook them, simply give them a good scrub and place them in well-salted cold water and slowly bring to the boil, allowing a good five minutes on the boil. Like lobsters their browny/bluish colour changes to a bright red when cooked. Drain and allow to cool. Open the crab, remove the gills and stomach sac (see page 14) and serve with bread and butter, salad leaves, a squeeze of lemon and a pair of nutcrackers.

Dressing a Lobster

Split the lobster along its length into two halves using a heavy knife with a sharp point. Remove the stomach sac, which you will find behind the mouth, and also the grey feathery gills located above the legs in the lower section of the body. Having removed the black thread of intestine from the tail section, the rest of the lobster is now entirely edible. You may wish to crack the claws to make it easier to extract the meat if you are serving whole lobster. The head of the lobster contains a creamy, light green/brown part, the 'tomalley' or liver, and if you have a hen lobster you may find a dark green 'coral', which are the roes, or eggs of the creature. Like crabs

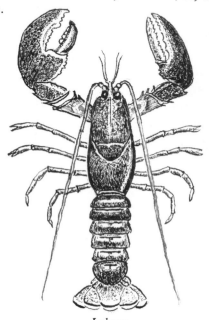

Lobster

female lobsters are distinguished by having wider tail parts, which serve to cover and protect the coral, which on cooking turns a glorious red colour. Both of these are much prized for their flavour and are usually extracted separately for beating into butter or cream to make hot or cold sauces to accompany the rest of the meat (see Chapter 5). Finally, use a little cooking oil to give a lustrous glaze to the shell of the lobster prior to serving.

Freezing Crabs and Lobsters

If you don't wish to eat the crab straight away you can freeze it in its shell, having removed the stomach, gills and tail parts. Wrap it well in a plastic bag, label it and store for up to two months in the freezer. You can do the same with lobsters. However, a better way to freeze whole lobsters is to place

16

them in a plastic drinks bottle with the neck cut off, topped up with fresh water, ensuring that the lobster will be completely encapsulated in a block of ice. This method is preferred to merely freezing in a plastic bag, where they can often develop a slight ammonia taste from the waste products excreted through the gills, even though you may have removed the stomach and gills. However, you can successfully freeze the white tail and claw meat in plastic bags once these parts are removed from the rest of the body and shell. Whichever method you choose, when you are ready to eat the shellfish, crab or lobster, slowly defrost it overnight in the fridge in a bowl which will allow the meat to drain and firm up to a nice meaty texture. Don't be tempted to defrost in a microwave as this will invariably produce a pappy result.

Edible Crab

CRAB RECIPES

Marinated Crabmeat Salad

Fish and chips and mushy peas may dominate traditional English seaside cuisine, but the crab salad tea must surely be its equal, and makes much healthier fare. Go to Cromer or Sheringham in late spring and you will find this superb dish made from the freshest ingredients on the menu of every local pub and restaurant for the rest of the summer. The following recipe however has a different pedigree and comes from Louisiana where the local Cajun cuisine, a spicy mixture of French and Creole cookery, knows a thing or two about shellfish in general and crabs in particular. The dish includes Tabasco sauce, which is only produced in Louisiana from spirit vinegar, salt, and chilli peppers grown on an island in the swamps, not far from Lafayette. In setting up the company the owner chose the location wisely, since the island sits atop a salt dome, providing an inexhaustible supply of seasoning. Although it does take a little longer to prepare, the results are worthwhile, served as a teatime treat or as a starter for a dinner party.

Ingredients

White meat from 2 or 3 large crabs
Quarter of a cup of olive oil
One large onion, chopped
3 tablespoons white wine vinegar
Several drops of Tabasco sauce
Half a teaspoon of English mustard powder
Pinch of thyme
Pinch of dried basil
2 tablespoons of freshly chopped parsley
2 tablespoons of limejuice
Salt and pepper
Head of lettuce torn into bite-size pieces

Parsley

Method

Combine all the ingredients, except for the crabmeat and lettuce, in a large bowl. Mix thoroughly and then gradually fold in the crabmeat, tossing lightly. Gently pack the mixture down and cover the bowl with cling film. Refrigerate for at least 4 hours giving it an occasional stir and pressing down.

Serving

When you are ready to serve remove from the fridge and toss in the torn lettuce at the last moment. Take immediately to the table. Serves 6-8.

NB Use up the leftover brown crabmeat to make shrimp and crab pâté.

Melon and Grapefruit Crab Starter

Served in a scooped-out half of melon this dish makes a simple and refreshing starter for a summer dinner party. It can be prepared well in advance and will happily sit in the fridge while the rest of the meal is being cooked.

Ingredients

12 ounces of cooked crabmeat (brown and white)
3 cantaloupe or honeydew melons
Grapefruit segments
Half a cup of mayonnaise (see p. 133 for a recipe)
A little olive oil
Lemon and/or lime juice
A head of chicory
Salt and pepper
Cayenne pepper
Almond flakes

Method

Mix the 'mayo', olive oil and lemon juice in a bowl and gently fold in the crabmeat and grapefruit segments, leaving the pieces of meat and fruit as large as possible. Adjust the seasoning to taste. Cool in the fridge and when you are ready cut the melons in half and scoop out the seeds. Spoon the crab mixture into the cavity, add a sprinkle of cayenne for colour and decorate with some long slices of chicory and the almond flakes. The recipe is just as delicious if you leave out the grapefruit.

Serving

Serve the melon on a plate with salad garnish and salt crackers. Serves 6.

LOBSTER RECIPES

Derek's Devilled Norfolk Lobster

The 'devil' in this recipe comes from the spicy and 'fiery' combination of good old Norfolk mustard and well-matured Cheddar cheese as a complement to the red and 'fiery' appearance of the lobster shell in which the dish is served.

Ingredients

One boiled lobster in its shell
One clove of garlic
One shallot
Cup of white wine
2 ounces of butter
Tablespoon of flour
Cup of milk
One teaspoon of Colman's mustard
Salt and Pepper
4 ounces grated Cheddar cheese

Garlic

Method

Cut the lobster in two from head to tail and carefully remove the meat from the shell and claws. Remove and discard the stomach sac and gills, reserving any coral or tomalley for the sauce. Cut the body meat into medallions about half an inch (12½ cm) thick. Scrub out the shells. Finely chop the garlic and shallot, soften in a small frying pan with half the white wine for around ten minutes. In the meantime make a simple white sauce by melting a knob of butter in a saucepan and gradually adding the flour and milk, constantly stirring. Finish the sauce by adding the rest of the wine and the sweated garlic and shallot. Reduce to a thick creamy sauce, adjust the seasoning and add the mustard to taste. Stir in any available coral or tomalley. Finally stir in most of the grated cheese and add the lobster meat, reserving some of the sauce for serving. Spoon the mixture back into the scrubbed-out lobster shells, sprinkle a little cheese on top and brown under the grill until the cheese bubbles.

Serving
Serve each sizzling lobster half on a hot plate; pour on the reserved sauce. Accompany with new potatoes and green beans to give an eye-dazzling array of colours, which perfectly complements the 'devilish' flavours. Serves 2.

Barbecued Lobster

Ingredients
Fresh lobster
Cup of olive oil
Half cup of lemon/lime juice

Method
Take a fresh lobster and kill it by the method described above. Cut it along its length into two halves using a heavy knife or cleaver and also crack the claw sections. Prepare a simple marinade of lemon juice and olive oil, brush onto the two lobster halves. Place on the well-heated grill, shell side down, for 5 minutes until the shell turns from blue to red and the flesh has set. Keep basting with the marinade, turn over and allow the hot bars of the grill to stripe lightly on the flesh side.

Serving
Salt sparingly and serve garnished with salad leaves, hot, crispy bread and your favourite well-chilled white wine.

Crab or Lobster Bisque

Having caught, cooked, dressed and then prepared your crab or lobster into any number of delicious dishes you may think, after all your hard work and grateful praise from your replete guests, that this is the end. But wait, for all that debris of broken shell, cracked claws, fiddly legs and hard-to-get-at shekel meat still contains a wealth of flavour which you can extract to give a power-packed soup to earn yet more plaudits for your culinary skill. And don't forget the humble shrimp or their bigger cousins the prawns, for their heads and tails can also be used in this recipe to add even more flavour. Add a little thickening to this basic soup and you can produce a delicious sauce to accompany almost any white fish and turn it into a gourmet dish of exceptional quality. You can of course add any spare crab, shrimp or lobster meat to the soup which will make it even more enjoyable, but shells alone will still make highly acceptable fare. This recipe is adapted from Jane Grigson's *Bisque de Homard* (Lobster Soup) where she notes 'crabs, shrimp, prawns and freshwater crayfish can all be used to make bisque, even the tiny crabs you pick up on holiday'. In other words, just about anything that climbs out of your shrimp net is fair game for this dish!

Ingredients

Edible crab or lobster debris
Shrimp or prawn heads and tails
Shore crabs
Velvet crabs
Any spare meat from the above
Whitefish leftovers.
2 carrots diced
One medium onion, roughly chopped
One celery stalk, chopped
6 tomatoes (and/or tomato purée)
2 cloves garlic thinly pared
Olive oil
Brandy
Half pint red wine
Half pint fish or meat stock (or stock cube and water)
Bouquet garni (bay, tarragon, sage, parsley etc.)
Salt, pepper, cayenne
Cream for serving

Garlic

Method

In a large heavy-based saucepan sweat the carrots, onion, celery and garlic in olive oil until soft. Add the shell debris, crabs etc. and cook until reddened; pour on a generous slug of brandy and set it alight. Now add the rest of the ingredients (except for the choice pieces of fish, crab meat etc.), ensuring there is sufficient liquid to just cover the contents. Put on the lid and bring to the boil, simmer for 40 minutes. Halfway through the cooking time, break up the debris (use a wooden rolling pin) to extract all the flavour; remove the lid to reduce and thicken. Pass the whole lot through a sieve and discard the debris, reserving any pieces of vegetable for inclusion in the final soup, and adding any spare crab, shrimp meat or leftover whitefish. (I usually dig out of the freezer any odd flatfish that need using up, microwave them for a couple of minutes and pick the best meat off the fillets.) Bring back to a final boil, taste and adjust the seasoning. Thicken with a little cornflour, or if you wish to make into a sauce, reduce further and then slowly add a flour and butter mixture *(beurre manière)* until the desired consistency is achieved.

Serving

Serve the soup or sauce with a swirl of cream and garlic olive oil croutons.

Shrimp and Crab Pâté

Ingredients

Boiled and peeled shrimps
Crabmeat-white or brown
Lobster meat
Melted butter (4ozs for every 12ozs of fish)

Grated nutmeg
Salt and pepper
Single cream if desired

Method
Blend the various meats or mash with a fork, reserving some whole shrimps and chunks of meat to give a coarser texture. Add all the other ingredients but reserve half the melted butter. Press the mixture into three or four small pots and allow to cool. Seal the pots with the remainder of the butter, add a curl of mace and a whole, unpeeled shrimp to identify the pot as a shellfish pâté. Freeze.

Serving
This is a good method of using up shellfish leftovers or odd bits of crab legs etc. The pâté freezes well and our family usually keep a couple of pots in reserve to serve as a starter to dinner on New Year's Eve. Eaten with thin pieces of toast the pâté offers an evocative taste of summer as the year turns. Serves 8-10

RICE WITH FISH AND SHELLFISH

Rice and shellfish make a particularly happy marriage and we can find wonderful recipes from countries around the world where rice is the staple crop. There is not too much rice grown in Norfolk at present but, who knows, with the threat of global warming this may become a possibility; until then we can still use locally caught marine fare to wonderful effect with the grain. In some dishes the rice makes a pleasant and interesting accompaniment to the fish or shellfish, and in these cases the use of wild rice, with its own distinctive nutty flavour, will admirably complement the dish. A mixture in the ratio of three parts white rice to one part wild rice can also be particularly tasty. In the following recipes long-grain white rice is used where it forms an integral part of the dish and the intention is that the rice should take on the flavours of the fish or shellfish itself. White rice comes in many varieties, with Basmati being universally recognised as the tastiest, but ordinary long-grain rice is quite suitable to achieve the desired effects. The rice may often be cooked prior to being incorporated into the dish; this method comes from an Egyptian friend who guarantees that it will always produce perfect results.

Toutou's Plain Boiled Rice

Ingredients
6 fluid ounces of plain white rice, wild rice or a mixture of both
8 fluid ounces of water (or stock)
Pinch of salt
Knob of ghee (clarified butter)

Method

In this method the quantity of fluid used is exactly one third more than the amount of rice. The quantities stated will be sufficient for two people, increase the quantities in the same proportions if you are cooking for more.

Put the rice in a pot with a close-fitting lid and pour on the already boiling water (or stock). Replace the lid and put to a low heat, or even better place in a moderately warm oven (the cool oven of an Aga is ideal). Cook for 15 minutes, avoiding the temptation to remove the lid. In this method the rice will slowly cook and swell to a fluffy softness, taking up all the water.

Serving

Simply stir the rice, adding if you wish a knob of butter or ghee.

Special Chinese Fried Rice

Any leftover crab and shrimp pâté makes an ideal base for this classic Cantonese dish. Chinese cuisine would approve of using 'leftover-leftovers' in this way, just so long as the colours and flavours of the resultant dish are in harmony. A well-balanced and harmonious Chinese dinner should contain all three 'meats', fish, poultry and pork or beef, a criterion met by this special fried rice. With its high oil content this dish is definitely not for slimmers, and in its native Canton is considered banquet fare of the highest order.

Ingredients
2 spring onions
3 eggs
2 ounces of smoked ham
4 ounces of shrimp or crab meat
4 ounces of green peas
4 cups of boiled rice
2 tablespoons soy sauce
Salt
Oil for cooking

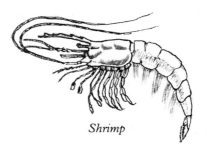

Shrimp

Method

Chinese cookery relies on fast cooking as a means of retaining freshness and flavour. In order to achieve this, all ingredients are chopped into small, similar-sized pieces to ensure that the heat is applied evenly (harmoniously the Chinese would say) so that they all cook through in the same time. This also means that the meals can be eaten with simple chopsticks, but in this case a spoon may be more useful. Make this dish in three parts as follows.

Pre-heat some of the oil in a wok or frying pan; meanwhile add half the spring onions to a bowl containing the lightly beaten eggs; add a pinch of salt and mix well. Scramble the eggs in the wok; when they are cooked remove and break them into small pieces with a fork. Keep them warm while you add more oil to the pan and stir-fry the diced ham, the shrimps or crab and the peas for about a minute. Remove, add more oil and repeat the process with the rest of the spring onions and the rice, stirring well to ensure that each grain of rice is coated with the oil to separate them. Reduce the heat, add the soy sauce and gradually mix in the rest of the cooked ingredients until all are evenly blended together.

Serving

Serve immediately as a light meal in its own right with a glass of chilled white wine, or as part of a multi-dish Chinese banquet.

Shellfish Risotto

Risotto comes from Italy (*riso* is Italian for rice) where the rice may be combined with a whole range of fish, meats and vegetables. The essential element is to cook the rice with the fish or meat stock so that it takes on all these flavours. Just about any shellfish, including cockles and mussels, can be used. One Italian speciality employs date mussels which actually bore into the rock of the seashore and can only be obtained by the use of a hammer and chisel!

Ingredients

One large onion finely chopped
One crushed clove of garlic
2 ounces of butter
Half a pound of long-grain rice (raw)
One pint of fish stock (or water and a stock cube)
6 ounces of peeled shrimps or prawns
Any spare crab or lobster meat (boiled)
Cockles and mussels (boiled)
Lemon slices

Method

Cook the onion and garlic gently in the butter until soft. Add the rice and continue to cook gently for a minute or two, stirring well. Add the stock and seasoning, bring to the boil, cover the pan and cook gently until most of the moisture is absorbed, then add the shellfish and continue to cook until the rice is really plump and tender and has absorbed all the moisture.

Serving

Sprinkle with grated cheese if preferred. Garnish with the lemon slices.

Paella

This classic Spanish dish is all about magnificence; magnificent aromas and flavours, magnificently contrasting colours and magnificent quantities, for traditionally the dish is made in a gigantic shallow pan intended to serve a hungry army. Even when you have this dish in a restaurant, any establishment worth its salt will insist that it is for a minimum of two people, and the act of sharing the multitude of tasty morsels that go to make up the dish is an important part of the gastronomic experience. The only essential ingredients are rice and saffron; just about anything that swims, walks, squawks or flies on or around the Iberian peninsula can go, or has gone, into a paella. You will have to go slightly beyond the limits of the Norfolk coast to find the ingredients that follow, but I promise it will be worth the effort, especially if you are catering for a large party where this dish will form a magnificent table centrepiece for everyone to help themselves.

Ingredients
One medium roasting chicken (with giblets)
One small lobster (boiled)
One medium sized squid
One pound of mixed shrimps and prawns (cooked but not shelled)
One pound of mussels in their shells
Half a pound of whitefish (cod, mullet, bass, haddock all go well)
Olive oil
One large onion finely chopped
Half a pound of tomatoes peeled and chopped (or a large tin of plum tomatoes)
Tomato paste
One teaspoon of paprika
3 cloves of garlic finely chopped
Salt and pepper
A little sugar
15 fluid ounces of white long-grain rice
Good pinch of saffron
6 ounces of shelled peas
One red pepper thinly sliced
3 lemons, wedged
3½ pints of water

Mussels

Method
You must allow for the fact that these ingredients take different times to cook, so start off by roasting the chicken and boiling the lobster; remove the meat from both and cut into chunks. Using the chicken carcase, giblets and lobster debris, start the stock pan going by adding them to the water, keeping it to a gentle simmer and adding other bits of debris and extra juices as they become available. Prepare the squid by removing the hard parts, ink sac and purplish skin, consign these to the stock pan and cut the head and tentacles into bite-sized pieces. Fillet the fish, season, and also cut into bite-sized pieces with the head, bones etc. going to the stock pan. Peel most of the shrimps and prawns, saving some whole for garnish, again putting the rubbish into the stock pan. Prepare the scrubbed and bearded mussels by steaming in their own juice in a heavy-based pan on a fierce heat; shell them (saving some in the shell for garnish) and strain the juices into the stock pan. Aim to get about a pint and three quarters of stock to complement the quantity of rice, adjusting the quantity by boiling off or diluting as appropriate (if you use more rice you will need more stock).

25

Now you are ready to start assembling and cooking the whole dish which should be undertaken in a wide shallow pan (the Spanish call it a *paellera*); something larger than one foot across is about right. If necessary, use two shallow pans rather than one deep one. With the stock still gently simmering in its pan cover the base of the *paellera* with olive oil and put to the heat to sweat the onions to a golden yellow, then add the tomatoes, tomato paste, garlic, and paprika to form a thick purée. If using English tomatoes, taste for sweetness and if necessary add a little sugar at this stage, this will also caramelise and add to the colour. Make room for the chicken pieces, brown them off and remove to a plate. Now add the rice and stir fry until transparent, then pour on half the strained stock and simmer gently. Take a cupful of stock in which to dissolve the saffron, and when the rice is half cooked return the chicken to the *paellera* and add the saffron, the fish and the remainder of the stock. After 10 minutes add the squid, then the vegetables, and finally, after another 5 minutes, add the cooked shellfish, giving the pan a shake to prevent sticking (stirring may prove to be too vigorous, try to avoid mashing the tender chunks of meat and fish). Finally add the prawns and mussels still in their shells, together with the lemon wedges, tucking them in and arranging them as an attractive garnish.

Serving
Take the *paellera* to the table in all its glory surrounded by more lemon wedges, a selection of different sorts of bread and large quantities of Spanish wine. Serves 10.

Cajun Shellfish Gumbo

The opening phrase of the Cajun folk song 'On the Bayou' runs 'jambalay, crawfish pie, filé gumbo,...' betraying the Louisianan origin of gumbo which is a thick, rich soup of fish and meat derived from the fusion of French and Créole cookery. Filé is a distinctive spice of the region made from the sassafras plant; it has a heavy, musky flavour. Every Cajun chef (which means just about every resident of Louisiana, for cookery is an all-consuming passion there) has his or her own recipe for gumbo, which as well as filé relies on the distinctive vegetable okra (Lady's Fingers) to provide body and thickening to the dish. If you can't find okra try a few slices of courgette for a close but not perfect substitute. I know of no substitute for filé but don't concern yourself to scour the local delis to find it, for the dish is still very tasty without it. The steamy Mississippi delta is ideal rice-growing country, which is why the dish is always served on a bed of plain rice; this may be steamed over the gumbo while it is cooking.

Ingredients
Half a cup of cooking oil
Half a cup of flour
2 large onions, sliced
2 green pepper, sliced
2 tablespoons of chopped parsley
2 cloves of finely chopped garlic
Can of plum tomatoes

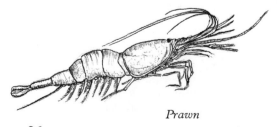

Prawn

26

Half a cup of chopped okra (or courgettes)
3 bay leaves
One teaspoon of thyme
A level teaspoon of cayenne pepper
2 tablespoons of lemon juice
4 whole cloves
Salt and pepper
6 thick slices of salami roughly chopped (or spicy sausage such as chorizo)
6 velvet crabs or two small edible crabs (cooked)
12 ounces of shelled shrimp or prawns
4 ounces of cockles/mussels/oysters (cooked and shelled)
2 pints of water
Cooked plain white rice
Chopped spring onions

Method
Heat the oil in a large heavy-based pan. Turn down to a low heat and gradually add the flour, stirring continuously until a medium brown roux is formed which will take about 20 minutes. Meanwhile, remove the stomach sacs from the crabs, divide into quarters and crack the claws. Add the onion, green pepper, parsley and garlic and sweat for a further 10 minutes until the vegetables are lightly browned. Season the mixture, add the water and okra, turn up the heat and boil for about one hour at a gentle simmer, adding the tomatoes, salami and shellfish about halfway through.

Serving
Serve in deep bowls half filled with plain boiled rice, sprinkle with the finely chopped spring onions. Provide warm crusty bread to mop up the spicy gravy (traditionally the Cajuns serve what they call biscuits which are made from cornmeal). Serves 4-6.

Shrimping

27

Cockling

Cockling is a wonderful way for a family to spend an afternoon; it has something for everyone. The kids will relish the opportunity to get covered from head to foot in mud, while the grown-ups will find great solace in sharing the magnificent open seascapes and balmy emptiness of the cockle beds with the oystercatchers, terns and other birds that inhabit these wild places. If you go in mid summer the endless beds of sea lavender with their purple flowers nodding in the breeze are a sight to be cherished, while the healthy exercise which the two-mile walk to the cockle beds will provide is another benefit. And at the end of a tiring day you will have the joy of a good meal and the satisfaction that comes from knowing you have collected your supper yourself.

Before you venture onto the sands there are some essential preparations to be made, for the tidal flats and creeks favoured by cockles *(Cardium edule)* can be dangerous places. First you will need to check the prevailing tides at your intended location. A 'phone call to the nearest harbourmaster can often provide the answer, or any fishing shop will supply a tide table for a few pence and give help in interpreting it if need be. You will only get out to the cockle beds at low tide, preferably on a low spring tide when the best beds will be exposed. And you will need to leave yourself plenty of time to collect your cockles and then get back before the incoming tide comes racing over the sands and up the creeks, cutting off the unwary from the shore. Avoid going after dark when you won't be able to see the hidden dangers, and more importantly no one will be able to see you. Aim to get to your beach about four hours after high tide, by which time the tide will be well down. This will give you two-three hours to stay on the sand; keep an eye on the time and make sure you leave the flats within two hours after the predicted time of low water.

Go dressed in your oldest clothes, well prepared to get muddy and wet. Take a broad-tined rake to scrape through the muddy sand (but often fingers prove best) together with a wicker basket to put your catch in. The basket allows you to give the cockles a swill round to get at least some of the sand and mud off them before putting them in the boot of the car, which should also advisedly be equipped with a plastic container of fresh water for getting all that mud off the kids before they get in the car. Towels are optional!

You will find countless small cockles; ignore these, the shells of the only ones worth eating will be at least an inch (25mm) across; three or four will fit pleasantly and comfortably into the palm of your hand. A good comparison is the satisfying feeling which a similar handful of walnuts provides, indeed in some parts of the country cockles are called sea-walnuts. If the cockle is partly open ignore these too, only tightly shut cockles will contain sound meat. Despite the apparent proliferation of Norfolk's cockle populations they are currently diminishing for a number of reasons, so a good rule is to take only enough for your own needs and no more. A good basketful of seven or eight pints of cockles will easily meet the needs of any of the recipes which follow, these have been designed to satisfy the appetites of for four or five hungry people.

Gathering Mussels

You will also find beds of mussels *(Mytilus edulis)* alongside the cockles on the banks of the creeks that wind over wide Norfolk beaches at places such as Stiffkey and Heacham. On the sand and shingle beaches further south and east, they live on the very ends of the groynes, hidden in crevices on those parts of the structures which are only exposed at the lowest tides. If you listen carefully you will hear a faint crackling sound as the mussels tighten up their shells awaiting the return of the tide, but you may also attract some odd looks from passers-by who wonder what on earth you are doing. A twenty-minute search, armed with an old fork, will easily produce enough for a meal for two, or starters for four. They are not very large but taste all the better for it. Take only the biggest and leave the tiddlers to grow on for another day. Mussels start spawning around late May through to early September during which time they are not really worth eating, and can be less efficient at filtering out unhealthy micro-organisms than in the colder months, so confine your collecting to when there's an 'r' in the month. Unlike cockles, which live under the sand, mussels live in colonies on rocks and stones in the tidal stream, which accounts for their highly streamlined shape. Living in this way makes them less liable to hold fine sand within their shells; several washings in plain water should remove any grittiness, but be aware of how persistent fine sand can be in sticking to cooking pans and utensils.

Basic preparations for cooking cockles

Having collected your cockles give them a thorough washing with plain water in a colander to get rid of the mud, sand and weed. Check them over, discarding any that are damaged, empty or not tightly shut. You can cook cockles straight away, having given them several washings in plain water, but the traditional treatment is to leave them to steep in salted cold water overnight. A light dusting of flour (and I do mean light, too

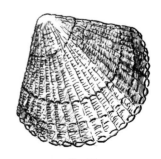

Cockle

29

much flour will result in a mouthful of wallpaper paste when you come to eat your cockles!) is usually added to encourage the cockles to filter the water and rid themselves of impurities. Aerating the water by occasionally dipping in a jug and splashing the water back into the container will aid the process. Recent legislation requires commercial cocklers to undertake an even more thorough cleansing process using ultra-violet light before offering them for sale. We all know that impurities from a variety of sources can contaminate our shorelines, so a modicum of common sense is required in avoiding the immediate vicinity of that suspicious pipeline which runs out to sea, but the essential precaution is to cook the shellfish at a temperature that will ensure that any micro-organisms are rendered harmless. Cook the cockles in a large saucepan, cover with a lid and bring to the boil on a high heat. There is no need to add any water to the pan, the cockles will open and simply stew in their own juice. Give them a good five minutes with at least three minutes at boiling point to ensure thorough sterilisation. Alternatively, place in a shallow dish and microwave for about five minutes on medium power. Remove from the heat, allow to cool and remove the shells. Wash thoroughly in a sieve; strain the cockle liquor to remove any fine sand.

If you are not going to use your cockles straight away they freeze well and will keep perfectly for six months. I usually put them into little glass paste pots with sealable lids, topping up the pot with some of the liquor but leaving space at the top to allow for expansion when frozen. Use them in fish soups, stock and as garnishes for other dishes.

BIVALVE RECIPES

Moules Marinières

This is a classic French dish, which the Belgians claim as a national dish and serve as a hot snack with mayonnaise and chips. Chez Léon, a famous family-run restaurant located in one of the busy alleyways surrounding Brussels' Grand Place, offers a bewildering and delicious number of versions of this humble fare, while the daily display of fish and shellfish by the dozens of neighbouring restaurants never fails to provide a colourful celebration of maritime fare. Whichever version you chose to prepare, always ensure that you serve the mussels in a communal pot, brimming over with the gaping dark blue shells dripping with creamy juices and steaming gently, for half the pleasure in eating them is to capture their steamy aroma and admire the intense colours of their shells. As with many such cheap, 'peasant' dishes presentation is everything.

Ingredients
30-40 mussels
One large onion

One-two cupfuls of white wine (but more will never hurt!)
Salt and pepper
Large dab of butter or dollop of double cream
Chopped parsley garnish
Homemade bread and butter

Method

Scrub the mussels well and remove the beards, discard any that are not tightly shut. Finely chop the onions and place with the mussels in a large saucepan. Cover with a lid and put straight on a high heat for the mussels to steam in their own juices for a good 8 minutes. Add the white wine and remove from the heat. Taste the milky juices, which will usually be quite salty, adjust the seasoning to your liking, and briskly stir in the butter or cream to enrich the gravy and glaze the deep blue mussel shells.

Serving

Serve in a communal pot with a parsley garnish providing each diner with a deep bowl and enormous chunks of warm bread. Use an empty shell to extract the meat, finish by drinking the soup, but beware of the inevitable slight trace of fine sand, which will be in the bottom of the bowl. Large napkins and finger bowls are advised. Serves 4-6 for starters, two as a main dish.

Variations

Shallots may be added, or substituted for the onion, as can leeks, which give a sweeter, milder flavour. Try using a good vintage cider instead of wine, but to achieve that authentic Gallic flavour add a clove of garlic and for a theatrical dinner party flourish serve with flaming brandy.

Limpets

Limpets *(Patella vulgata)* are those conical shells that you find attached to rocks when on holiday in Devon or Cornwall, but not surely in Norfolk? Well these days you do find limpets in Norfolk as a result of the Environment Agency's efforts, in the early 1990s, to reduce coastal erosion by placing enormous rock groynes and reefs out to sea, especially in the Sea Palling area. It didn't take long for limpets to colonise these reefs, where they now thrive. But are they any good to eat? Well the answer is a cautious yes, and you will certainly find them as an integral part of an *Assiette de Mer*, especially in Brittany where they are highly regarded. They were certainly enjoyed by our forebears as archaeologists confirm from the large number of waste heaps (middens) of limpet and oyster shells discovered at prehistoric sites. Like cockles they can be gritty, and like whelks they can be rubbery, but aficionados claim they are 'real seafood, with a flavour which encapsulates the essence of salt-wind, spume and sunshine!' If you want to collect limpets there are a number of things you need to know. First, you will

31

need to visit the reefs at low tide when the rocks are fully exposed. Secondly, you must be aware that the reefs are dangerous places and you must exercise great care in approaching them, for they are covered in any number of species of extremely slippery seaweeds. Climbing on top of the reefs is only for the foolhardy; you will find plenty of limpets at the base of the rocks, easily accessible from the sands. The third thing you need to know is that the limpet doesn't like being gathered for food, and at low tide it returns from foraging to its normal resting place and attaches itself very, very firmly to its rocky perch. In fact it does this so well that breaking the shell is the only way of removing them, unless you are patient. For after a while the limpet relaxes its grip and raises itself slightly from the rock surface, and it is at this time that you, or a passing tern or oystercatcher, can secure a meal. Give the limpet a sudden, and unannounced, sideswipe with a knife or old fork and the prize can be yours. But be warned, the slightest touch to the creature will announce your intentions and it will stick firm, but if you do make a mistake, just move on to the next rock and try your luck again.

Limpet Pie

Ingredients
30-40 limpets
Mashed potato
Bacon pieces
Butter
Milk
Fish stock
Salt and pepper
Grated cheese

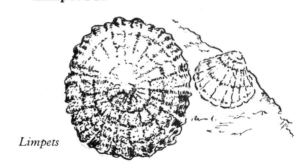
Limpets

Method
If you have time you can use the cockle method to cleanse the limpets; if not scrub them well and proceed as follows. Boil the limpets in salted water (or a little fish stock) for about ten minutes. Remove them from the shells, pulling out the two little horn-like tentacles. They are now ready to eat. To make them tastier, finely chop or mince them and then fry with the chopped bacon in the butter for about three minutes, adding a little milk, fish stock and flour to make a thin sauce. Layer the mixture in a casserole dish with the mashed potato. Furrow the top layer of potato with a fork and sprinkle with a little cheese. Place in a hot oven and heat through until the potato is nicely browned.

Serving
Serve with roasted vegetables. Serves 6.

Norfolk Shellfish and Samphire Platter

As any Francophile will tell you, a trip to Normandy or Brittany would not be complete without an evening in a fish restaurant enjoying an *Assiette de Mer*. Typically, a wide variety of shellfish go to make up this classic dish including freshly boiled crabs, mussels, oysters, cockles, winkles, shrimps and, if you're lucky, a few chunks of lobster and some enormous prawns.

Ingredients for six people
6 small-medium edible crabs
6 velvet crabs
One or two lobsters
6 oysters
30 mussels
6 whelks
30 cockles
30 winkles
2 pints (about one pound) of unpeeled shrimps
12 large prawns
Lemon wedges
Samphire - see below
Ice cubes
Fresh bread
Bottle(s) of wine

Method
Either buy your boiled shellfish from the fishmonger or prepare as described elsewhere. Allow to cool and refrigerate well prior to serving.

Serving
Traditionally served on a bed of iced seaweed (for seaweed see p. 123) and lemon wedges, this celebration of the sea comes complete with a comprehensive tool-kit of forks, lobster picks, nutcrackers and glass-headed pins (for the winkles). A large well-starched linen napkin and a finger bowl each will be appreciated by your guests. Suitably equipped, you may spend a glorious couple of hours extracting the goodness from the shells of the creatures, all accompanied by a variety of mayonnaise dips, a bottomless wine carafe, crusty French bread and scintillating conversation. Serves 6.

Shelling a prawn

Removing the tail shell

Twisting off the head

Peeling off the body tail

For a Norfolk *Assiette de Mer*, let's call it a shellfish platter, the same array of tantalising morsels is readily available, but here in the 'mysterious East' we have an extra ingredient that adds yet more delight to the feast. Instead of serving the dish on a bed of seaweed, substitute the local speciality of marsh samphire *(Salicornia europaea)*. Samphire (pronounced 'samfer') is a maritime plant, a glasswort that grows on the salt marshes of the north Norfolk coast and is often referred to as 'Norfolk asparagus'. The name samphire derives from the French *herbe de St Pierre* Eaten in a similar way to globe artichoke, by stripping off the fleshy parts between the teeth, the vegetable has a wonderfully delicate taste of the sea, a taste which can easily be lost if smothered in vinegar, which is how it is often served accompanied by bread and butter. Using it as a basis for a shellfish feast is far preferable; use a little lemon juice if you wish to sharpen the taste.

Preparing Samphire
First collect your samphire, either the hard way by searching the marshes off Blakeney, Cley or Salthouse suitably armed with a garden fork, a bag, a good botanical field guide and a tide-table, or preferably by buying a large bag of the stuff for a modest outlay from one of the many cottage back doors in these villages that specialise in this sort of thing.

Ingredients
One pound of samphire (half a pound per person)
Plain water
Butter
Pepper

Samphire

Method
Give the plants a thorough washing, trim the roots and steam in a colander over briskly boiling water for around ten minutes. Check for tenderness and seasoning (careful with the salt; it will naturally be quite salty). Add a knob of butter.

Serving
Serve immediately with a mayonnaise dip and bread and butter. For a seafood platter allow to cool and spread out on the plate, piling your shellfish on top. Add ice and lemon wedges and serve. Serves 2.

See Chapter 5 for samphire sauce and mayonnaise dip.

Spaghetti Alla Vongolese

This dish is based on a classic Italian speciality that uses tellins, a thin-shelled mollusc, as the basis for seafood spaghetti. You won't find tellins in collectable quantities on the Norfolk coast, but you will of course find cockles, which are an excellent substitute.

Ingredients
5 pints of cockles in their shells (or one pint of cooked cockles)
2 large onions
2 pounds chopped tomatoes and a tablespoon of tomato purée
2 thick rashers of bacon per person
Clove of garlic
Olive oil
2 bay leaves
Flour or cornflour seasoned with salt and pepper
Spaghetti
Parmesan cheese

Cockle

Method
Prepare and cook the cockles in the normal way. Fry the bacon, garlic and onions in olive oil until browned, place in a casserole. Add the other ingredients including the cockles and the strained liquor. Cook in a moderate oven for 30 minutes, remove the lid for the last 10 minutes to reduce the liquid. Add a knob of butter and a little flour or cornflour to thicken the sauce.

Serving
Boil the spaghetti in the usual way and serve with the sauce. Add grated cheese.

Breakfast Cockles

We don't usually think of having fish for breakfast beyond the traditional kippers and, with the exception of kedgeree, I know of no other breakfast shellfish dish. So, this somewhat unusual breakfast, which comes from Wales, undoubtedly stems from a practical cook's efforts to ensure that good food is never wasted, a philosophy well realised in this simple, and salty combination of land and sea ingredients.

Ingredients
8 ounces of streaky bacon
8 ounces of cockles (cooked & shelled)
A little fat or oil

Method
Chop the bacon into small pieces and gently fry with the cockles for 4-5 minutes. Serve with scrambled eggs on toast.

Loaves and Fishes – a Word about Bread

You will find among these recipes many that include some form of bread as an accompaniment, for the combination of fish and bread is a delight discovered very early in history. When you serve bread with fish, it is worth taking care to select the most suitable form of bread, and to serve it at its best, which essentially means fresh, crusty and hot. Some supermarkets do offer a range of tasty specialist breads, but here in the UK we still lag behind our continental cousins in the variety and quality on offer. The very existence of the supermarket has caused the traditional baker to become a rarity on the High Street. However, the invention of the home bread-maker has enabled anyone to bring delicious fresh bread to the table whenever it is required. Personally I find measuring precisely the basic ingredients of flour, yeast, sugar, water etc. an exacting task, for the amounts must be absolutely correct to ensure success. It is far better to experiment with the many ready-prepared bread mixes on offer and, having found one or two to your taste, stick with them, adding if you wish other ingredients such as whole grains or chopped dried fruits to ring the changes. If you are planning a fishy dinner party, you can please your guests by serving hot bread straight from the oven, and if the 'oven' is actually the bread-maker, carefully set to complete its cycle as the fish is ready to serve then nobody need be any the wiser.

If you don't own a bread-maker you can always freshen up a bought loaf by splashing a little cold water over it and putting it in a hot oven for a couple of minutes. Toasting very thin slices for five minutes in a hot oven will produce **Melba toast**; whilst thicker 'doorsteps' drizzled with olive oil and sprinkled with mixed herbs to produce **Italian crostino** will take a little longer. Bread rolls can be split and slowly baked in a cool oven to produce crispy rusks; in Norfolk we call them **Hollow Biscuits**. All of these make ideal bases for fish pâtés, marinated fillets or shellfish moistened with a little mayonnaise. Cubes of bread may be shallow-fried in oil (with or without garlic) to produce **croutons** to add to soups or as a tasty salad garnish. Finally, don't forget the role of breadcrumbs, which are best made from stale bread (it crumbles better) and are used in a number of ways in fish cookery. As a crispy coating for long thin fillets of fried fish, breadcrumbs serve to protect the fish from the fierce heat long enough to allow the flesh to cook, and most importantly to stay moist; the fact that the breadcrumbs also absorb some of the fat adds considerably to the flavour, and the calories! However, as long as you call them **goujons** rather than fish fingers your guests will be suitably impressed, and doubly so if you tell them that you made the bread yourself. Breadcrumbs form the basis of pâtés made from fish roe such as taramasalata and they are also used to make stuffing or

36

forcemeat. The following recipe with its many variations can be used for a wide variety of both round and flatfish.

Forcemeat Stuffing for Fish

Ingredients
2-3 ounces soft breadcrumbs (remove the crusts before zapping in a blender)
2 ounces of melted butter
2 teaspoons of lemon juice
Grated lemon rind
2 teaspoons finely chopped parsley
Grate of nutmeg
Salt and pepper
Lightly beaten egg
Serves 4

Method
Mix the dry ingredients in a bowl and fold in the melted butter; add enough beaten egg to form a stiff mixture. Stuff the stomach cavity of round fish, securing the flaps with cocktail sticks. Don't overfill; the breadcrumbs will swell with cooking and the fish may split if too full and look unsightly on the plate. Flat fish can be stuffed by making long cuts alongside the backbone and stuffing the pockets that are formed. Fillets may be rolled around a cylinder of stuffing, or use two fillets to make a forcemeat sandwich, securing all with cocktail sticks. Removing the bone from a fish steak will leave a cavity suitable for stuffing. For lobster, mix the stuffing with the boiled and coarsely-chopped lobster meat, put the mixture back in the shell for grilling. Baking in foil is the preferred method for cooking stuffed fish; use any leftover forcemeat to thicken the juices for a sauce.

Variations
Add finely chopped onion that has been sweated in oil until soft and clear, or chopped chives for a more delicate flavour. Garlic cloves may be too overpowering in forcemeat, but try seasoning with a little garlic salt. Herb variations can include basil, fennel or dill. Finely chopped, boiled shellfish (shrimps, prawns, mussels) will add both flavour and texture as will poached and sieved roes, but be careful for they can overpower the other flavours. Small quantities of chopped grapes, figs and apricots, or their dried forms such as sultanas or raisins provide contrasting flavours, as will shreds of dried lemon or orange peel. Finally, fish stock, wine or cider can all be used as alternative moistening agents, and plain boiled rice may be used as a groundmass instead of breadcrumbs.

CHAPTER TWO
SUMMER

'In a bowl to sea went wise men three,
On a brilliant night in June:
They carried a net, and their hearts were set
On fishing up the moon'.
The Wise Men of Gotham. *Paper Money Lyrics*
Thomas Love Peacock (1785-1866)

As the storms of winter fade and the seas become more benign the longshoreman turns to a different method of catching the summer visitors that come to our shoreline. Tangle netting involves anchoring a large transparent mesh net to the seabed across the stream of the current. At each end of the net short sticks, weighted with lead, hold the net nearly upright so that it acts like an underwater fence. Locally these are called 'Dan Lenos', a corruption of *guindineaux,* the French name for this piece of equipment (Dan Leno was actually an Edwardian music hall artist). The net is put out with a moderate tide running, in a similar way to a shank of crab pots, to ensure that the lead anchor gets a good grip on the seabed so that the net remains firm. Marked with dahns it is left for one or two tides and retrieved at slack water, by which time any number of sea creatures, and usually quite a lot of seaweed and other debris, will have become entangled in the net. Either in the boat or back on the shore the patient longshoreman will remove his catch, which may include crab, lobster, skate, sea bass, gurnard, mullet, dogfish, cod and any variety of flatfish, all creatures that scavenge on the sea floor for their fare. Patience is certainly needed, for crabs will become hopelessly tangled in the net; their strong pincers will also cause damage to the nets, which will need to be repaired before setting again. The tangle nets are made from a single mesh of tough monofilament, but an even deadlier variation of the tangle net is the trammel net. This comprises three layers of net, a central sheet of smaller-meshed net flanked on both sides by a much larger-meshed net usually of different coloured filament. This net is similarly anchored to the seabed and will catch the larger species of fish when they become trapped in the central layer, which then pushes through either of the larger side meshes, forming an inescapable pocket. Trammel nets are particularly effective at catching skate.

Seine netting is yet another netting technique, but this is controlled from the shore. The net, usually about a fathom in depth, is fitted with a heavy bottom rope, which contains strands of lead to weigh it down. The seine is then set in a semicircle just offshore, either by rowing it out in a dinghy or by wading in as deep as the longshoremen can go. Attached to each end of the

Seine-fishing

net are two long ropes (tows), which are brought back to the shore. The net is allowed to drift slowly down with the tide and, when ready, the ropes on either end are used to pull the net towards the beach, carefully maintaining it in an ever-decreasing semicircle. I have seen this done on Southern Indian beaches using heavy coir (coconut fibre) nets and ropes where the net is set up to a quarter of a mile offshore and it takes teams of twenty men an hour or more to haul it in. As the net is hauled into the shallows of a Norfolk beach, the heavy lead line scrapes along the bottom, trapping any bottom-dwelling flatfish, whilst the semicircle of the net or the mesh itself captures the swimming fish such as mackerel, grey mullet or sea trout. A traditional technique to stop the entrapped swimming fish jumping over the top of the net is to sprinkle sawdust just in front of it; this dissuades the fish from breaking the surface. With care the two ends of the net are brought closer together to form a bag, which is finally hauled up the beach where the catch is removed.

On a calm sunny day, sea trout are one of the real prizes of seine net fishing and this technique is particularly favoured in wide estuaries to capture these superb fish as they migrate up river to spawn. However, there are few such wide estuaries on the Norfolk coast although the west Norfolk River Wissey, a tributary of the Great Ouse, does boast a small run of sea trout in its chalky upper reaches. I suspect that many of the Norfolk coastal sea trout are captured when they come close inshore to bask in the shallows to rid themselves of the small black sea lice that attach themselves to their flanks.

As high summer approaches, the mackerel *(Scomber scombrus)* will start to appear near our shores, their presence traditionally heralded by the gulls

39

diving to feed both on the mackerel, and the whitebait upon which the mackerel themselves are feeding. Mackerel can be caught in the same way as herring, using slightly larger-meshed nets, or by trolling with a rod and line. This method involves keeping the boat moving slowly through the water, trailing a line fitted with half a dozen hooks and feathers. Some people use shiny pieces of kitchen foil instead of feathers; whatever you use, the fast swimming mackerel are attracted by the lure and grab at it, thus getting hooked in the process. When this happens the resultant jerk on the rod and line leaves the fisherman in little doubt that he has achieved his aim; it is not unusual to get a fish on every hook. Having located a shoal, the boat may be anchored or allowed to drift with the tide and the lines dropped vertically overboard, slowly raising the line up and down to ensure that the hooks are presented at the depth at which the mackerel are feeding. A good haul will see eighty to a hundred caught in a couple of hours, especially off the north coast of Norfolk at places like Brancaster and Cley, where the best shoals are usually found. But be warned, if the sky is threatening rain don't bother searching for the mackerel, for as soon as the rain falls and reduces the salinity of the seawater, the mackerel will disappear to saltier climes.

Catching the fish and landing them calls for a good deal of hard work, but preparing the fish for the kitchen is much easier; with just a little practice and the right tools, anyone can master the secrets of the fishmonger's cutting slab.

Basic Preparation for Flat Fish

The following method works well for all flatfish such as soles, dabs, plaice or flounders. Gut the fish by making a one-inch (25mm) diagonal cut from just behind the head to the base of the dorsal fin. Remove the guts and clean the fish; remove the head and fins (leave the head on smaller fish and on those you intend to skin). You can now cook the fish in this state, or if preferred skin and fillet it using the following method.

Skinning

Lay the fish on a board with the dark skin upward and the head facing away from you. Grip the fish by its tail (use a pinch of salt to get a better grip if necessary) and make a shallow cut across the skin of the tail with a good sharp knife, keeping the knife flat and easing up the skin to provide a decent bit to get hold of. Gripping the skin, tear it from the fish, using the knife to hold the fish flat and help ease the skin from the flesh as it comes away. If you wish, remove the white skin under the fish in the same way.

Preparing Flatfish

1. *Slitting skin above the tail*

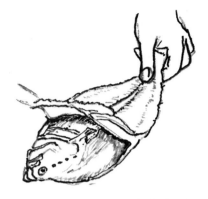

2. *Drawing skin towards the head*

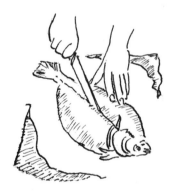

3. *Cutting down the backbone*

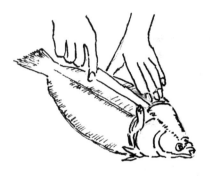

4. *Slitting just below the head*

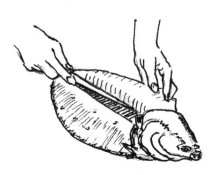

5. *Separating fillet from the bone*

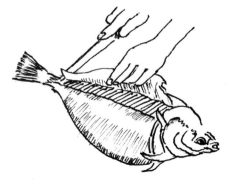

6. *Removing the second fillet*

Filleting

Four quarter-cut fillets can be obtained from a flat fish, two from each side. Lay the fish dark side up with the head away from you. Use the point of the knife to cut in a straight line down the middle of the back from head to tail. Using a similar technique to the skinning process, fillet the fish by lifting the flap of flesh and, keeping the knife flat, cut in a slicing motion towards the side of the fish just above the pin bones, using them as a guide. You may need to make a couple of sweeping cuts, giving a small jerk to the knife finally to release the fillet. Having removed the fillet from one side, you can repeat for the other side; if necessary turn the fish round with the tail away from you and cut from tail to head, turning the knife up slightly as you reach the head to remove the fillet completely. Turn over and remove the other two fillets; trim them as necessary. Use a similar technique if you want to form a pocket to stuff the fish but don't completely remove the fillet. Smaller fish may yield only one cross-cut fillet from each side giving two per fish.

Skinning Small Flatfish - another method

I saw this method in a small holiday resort on the Baltic coast of Poland where three or four boats were tied up to the quay and the nets, full of fish, were being slowly cleaned out on the quayside. Most of the catch comprised flounders, and as soon as the fishermen (and fisher girls) removed the fish from the net they were being filleted and sold directly to the holidaymakers who gathered eagerly around the boats. They dealt with the fish as follows.

With a razor-sharp knife the fins and lateral pin bones of the fish were removed, using a sawing technique to cut down each side. The body of the fish was held firmly on the board with the part to be removed (a good half inch along each flank to be sure of getting all the tiny bones) hanging over the side. The fish was then turned on its back and cut across the base of the tail through the flesh and bone, down to, but not through, the dark skin. Grasping the tail, the filleter bent it back, making it a handle to tear off the dark skin back towards the head, using his thumb to help part the skin from the body of the fish. He then removed the head with a semicircular cut, at the same time drawing out the guts and the remnant of dark skin. The chap I saw took about ten seconds per fish, but I guess he had had a lifetime of practice. The fish now contained only the easily removable larger bones and white skin, and could be prepared in a number of ways, including smoking, for the boats were also offering smoked flounder, a Baltic delicacy rarely found in this country but well worth trying.

42

Basic Preparation for Round Fish

Set out your 'stall' by spreading several sheets of newspaper over the work top next to the sink and placing a wooden chopping board in the middle. With a pair of kitchen scissors remove any fins and spines; on a bass I also usually snip off the row of barbs found on the gill covers. Scale the fish using a knife or de-scaler working from the tail towards the head. Scales will fly everywhere especially when using a de-scaler. I find a controlled action with the knife held at a shallow angle more effective at retaining the scales but inevitably some will end up on the other side of the kitchen. Slit the belly from just behind the head towards the tail and remove the guts and any roes (which may be saved for other tasty dishes). Cut through the gut near the throat, scraping out the internal organs and other membranes. Open the cavity and run a knife along both sides of the backbone to clear the blood vessel that you will find there. In sea trout this blood vessel is quite thick and a strong teaspoon can be used to scrape it out, followed by a good scrub with a stiff brush to remove all of it from the indentations in the backbone. Give the inside of the fish a thorough wash under running water and decide whether or not to remove the head or tail. In removing the head, follow the line of the gills in a semicircular cut so as not to leave any more good meat on the head than necessary; finally chop straight across the back of the head to sever the backbone.

Cleaning through the Gills

Splitting the fish through the belly can spoil its appearance and also causes the roe to be removed at the same time, which is undesirable in the case of herring being prepared for the Scotch Cure. The alternative is to gut the fish through the gills, something that the Scotch fisher girls did to herring at the rate of one per second for hours on end. To release the gut at its lower end, make a small incision at the bottom of the belly by the vent and snip through the end of the innards. Then cut through the bone under the lower jaw, open the gills' flaps and, inserting your knife and thumb into the cavity, gently grasp and tease out the innards.

Fish Steaks

Round fish are not usually skinned prior to cooking, except for the dogfish which requires some quite heavy duty tools to persuade the creature to part with its skin (see p. 66) If you wish to prepare fish steaks, cut around the body of the fish at one inch (25mm) intervals using a very heavy knife on a

Preparing Round Fish

1. *Loosening skin below the head*

2. *Drawing the skin towards the tail*

3. *Cutting along the backbone*

4. *Removing the backbone*

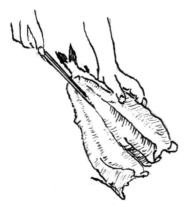

5. *Freeing the first fillet*

6. *Cutting off the tail*

board; chop through the backbone by banging down on the back of the knife. Leave the last five inches (13cm) or so nearest the tail as a whole piece. Scrape down the board onto the newspaper and wrap up the offal for disposal. (I usually throw it back into the sea to feed the crabs.) Sea bass, grey mullet, salmon, sea trout, herring, cod, whiting, mackerel etc. may all be prepared in this way for cooking as whole fish, or filleted as follows (usually mackerel are filleted from the bone).

Filleting Round Fish

You can cut two fillets from a round fish, one from each side. To fillet a round fish you will need a medium-size kitchen knife, which must have a flexible blade to allow you to follow the natural contours of the fish. It also goes without saying that your knife needs to be sharp; use a steel to give it a good edge to make the job easier, and safer.

Lay the fish on its side on the board and, starting at the head end, cut across the fish with a sawing motion down towards the backbone. Before the knife comes into contact with the backbone, cut and turn it through ninety degrees so that the blade is parallel to the backbone, and continue cutting towards the tail in a continuous sawing motion to remove the fillet. With a little practise you will soon become expert at removing a good-sized fillet leaving a minimum of flesh adhering to the backbone. Turn the fish over and remove the other fillet in the same way. It may be easier to bone out a large round fish by gutting in the normal way and then cutting either side of the backbone from within the cavity. Carefully lever out the backbone by sliding the knife underneath it, bringing with it as many of the pin bones as possible. This method is particularly effective for preparing sides of sea trout for smoking. Any remaining pin bones can be removed with tweezers. Use a slightly different technique for herring by placing the beheaded and gutted fish right way up on the board and firmly pressing with your thumb along the back, flattening the fish. Turn over and carefully tease out the backbone, leaving a boned double fillet.

Butterflying Round Fish

Butterflying is a method of preparing a round fish by flattening it to give an even thickness, something which makes it much easier to handle and turn when grilled or barbecued, especially if you use one of those hinged metal grills made for the purpose. An equal thickness means that the fish will cook more evenly and you will avoid having the tail end burned to a crisp and the thicker head end practically raw. The cutting process is identical to kippering, where the whole herring is cut down the backbone and opened up like a book to remove its guts. With a larger fish, such as sea trout or salmon, the best technique is to remove the head and tail completely and draw the guts from the cavity, resisting the temptation to slit the belly. Instead, insert the knife into the back about a third of the way along its length and slice alongside the backbone towards the tail, sweeping the knife out at the end. Go back into the cut and do the same thing in the opposite direction. You will inevitably cut through many of the pin bones but these can subsequently be removed with fingers or a pair of tweezers. The 1508 *Booke of Kerving* suggests the verb 'to chine' is the proper term for carving a salmon for the table, where the word chine means the spine or backbone. Open the fish out into its butterfly shape and chine the fish by sliding the knife under the backbone, lifting and easing it from the flesh. The purpose of kippering is to expose as much of the herring's flesh as possible to the smoke; butterflying is about exposing as much flesh as possible to an even heat. Of course it is highly appropriate to butterfly salmon, for the word kipper actually originates from the practice of smoking these fish. In the breeding season the jaw of a male salmon develops a bony projection, a 'kip', by which it battles with other males to secure a mate. In former times these spent 'kipper salmon' were readily captured but not the best of eating, and so they were smoked, or kippered, to improve their flavour and preserve this glut of fish that came at the end of the breeding season. Gradually the term became applied to other smoked fish, especially the herring.

Icing and Freezing Fish

The practice of using ice to preserve fish and stop it deteriorating had its origins in Norfolk, for in the late winter of 1822 William Leftwich (1770-1843) despatched a charter vessel from Great Yarmouth to Norway which returned in the May of that year laden with 300 tons of fjord ice. This early pioneer of frozen food technology was interested in the dairy rather than the fishing industry, but the advantages of ice as a preservative were well recognised by local fishermen, fishing fleet owners and fishmongers alike, who all encouraged the practice. This was especially true of Samuel Hewett, owner of the Gorleston-based Short Blue Fleet of fishing luggers, who revolutionised the fishing industry by developing the fleet method of fishing. Hewett kept his luggers at sea for long periods, fishing continually, transferring the catches in fish trunks to much faster cutters which raced for the London markets to secure the best prices. It was only the use of ice for packing the trunks that made this possible. Incidentally, the catches were sorted into two categories, prime and offal, with the former comprising soles, brill, turbot and halibut, whilst the offal consisted of plaice, cod, haddock, whiting and anything else!

Leftwich made a tidy profit from his initiative and the importation of Norwegian ice, the 'ice trade', became an essential part of Great Yarmouth's economy, and common practice throughout Victorian England. In the harsher winters of the late 19th century, ice broken from frozen Broads was regularly brought by trading wherries to the town to supplement overseas imports, which struggled to meet demand. The ice was stored and kept frozen in well insulated, specially built, thatched ice-houses from where it was sold to be taken on board the fishing boats for use at sea, or used for boxing landed fish in ice for subsequent export to Germany. There is a superb example of a fully restored ice-house just by Great Yarmouth's Haven Bridge. Towards the end of the century ice-making factories that used the physical principles of heat exchange to produce refrigeration and thus create ice from fresh water, eventually replaced the ice trade. It was no accident that the 20th century pioneer of frozen food, Clarence Birdseye, established a food factory in Great Yarmouth in 1945, having developed the refrigeration process to freeze food directly. By the 1950s the domestic refrigerator, and soon after the domestic freezer, became universally available and the art of home freezing was born; ready-made frozen products, such as Birdseye Fish Fingers, first invented and developed by the company in Gt. Yarmouth, soon followed.

There is one simple rule to remember when freezing fish, which is that the process of freezing slows down, but cannot wholly prevent the fish deteriorating. This means that if the fish goes into the freezer shortly after being pulled from the sea, the resultant deterioration will be slight, and I have successfully frozen and kept whitefish such as mullet or bass for a couple of years with little significant change in taste or texture. The same is not true for oily fish where, even with freezing, the oil they contain will fairly quickly turn rancid and spoil the flavour. Three months is all right, six months is a maximum for herring, mackerel or sprats, even when smoked. Shop-bought fish, will never be as fresh as that which you catch yourself, and as a result freezer times are considerably shortened to just a few weeks, or even days.

There are a number of techniques for freezing fish but, with very few exceptions, all fish should be gutted and scaled prior to storage. It is also important to wrap the fish in some sort of protective coating which will exclude as much air as possible from the package, and also be thick enough to prevent freezer burn, which dries the flesh of the fish and makes it tough and tasteless. Whole fish will usually keep better than steaks or fillets, but the wise cook will seek a balance between storing whole fish or portions, given the convenience that the latter afford.

When I catch bass, mullet or sea trout in quantity, I will gut and scale the fish as soon as possible, for after a few hours the scales becomes far more difficult to shift and the extra force needed to remove them will cause them to fly all over the kitchen. Snip off the fins and thoroughly clean the fish inside and out to remove all traces of blood, especially along the backbone. Rinse the fish through the mouth and gills and allow to drain for a few minutes, and then proceed to fillet or steak the fish if required. Place the whole fish, or portions, in a clean plastic bag, wrapping carefully and tightly so that the plastic clings to the flesh and removes as much air as possible. Having produced a neat plastic bundle, wrap it again in another bag and secure the package with stout elastic bands. Label and date with a waterproof marker pen and place in the freezer. Treat flat fish in a similar way, again carefully double-wrapping to prevent freezer burn.

Oily fish respond well to ice glazing where the ungutted fish are repeatedly dipped in fresh water and allowed to freeze to produce a thin layer of ice which encapsulates the fish. However, this method is too time-consuming for storing large quantities of herring or mackerel and I resort to the double plastic bag method, having first gutted and scaled the fish. Sprats are too fiddly to be gutted prior to freezing and are usually frozen whole. Freezing whole fish or shellfish in block ice using old plastic drinks bottles can be very successful.

Defrosting, especially larger whole fish, should be done slowly in the refrigerator, usually overnight and throughout the next day. Any attempt to speed up the process by exposure to heat in say, a microwave, will usually mean that the cellular structure of the flesh will be broken down and the fish will become water saturated, with a drastic loss of flavour and texture. Thin fillets of white fish, or small stuff like sprats can be successfully cooked direct from frozen, but don't try it with thick fish steaks.

Freezing has revolutionised the fish industry, resulting in a much wider variety of species, such as hoki or red snapper, which are caught in far-off waters, now being available for the table and obtainable from local shops. For the successful Norfolk longshoreman, however, the greatest benefit has been that the boom-and-bust nature of fishing, large catches one day followed by days or weeks of blanks, can now be accommodated, and eating fresh fish on a regular basis has become the norm.

Sea Bass

SUMMER FISH RECIPES

Dover Sole with Asparagus Sauce

Wimbledon fortnight may hold no great attraction for a Norfolk longshore fisherman, but it does coincide with a culinary delight to rival strawberries and cream. For the month of June is when the Dover sole *(Solea solea)*, known locally as 'slips', come close inshore to feed on the shrimps that also cling close to the warm, plankton-rich waters lapping onto the summer beach. Unlike dabs or flounders, the Dover sole needs no help from the brown shrimp to take its place at the head of the list of sweetest fish, for it is widely regarded as the best flavoured of the smaller flatfish, but only if you are patient. Scientific research has confirmed that the chemical substances that provide these agreeable flavours quickly break down in most other flatfish to produce the noxious smells that we associate with stale fish. In contrast, these same substances and flavours in the sole only fully develop after the fish has been caught, and for the best flavour soles should be allowed to mature in the fridge for a few hours in order to be at their best. Another culinary gem also reaches its prime in early June in the shape of the intense green spears of asparagus, a vegetable supremo that favours lighter, well-drained sandy soils and can often be found growing wild in the dunes close to the seashore. Not surprisingly, soles and asparagus have unerringly found their way onto the same plate, evoking the very essence of summer, just as surely as Wimbledon's strawberries and cream.

Ingredients
Fresh sole fillets
Lemon juice
Salt and pepper
Asparagus sauce (see p.137)

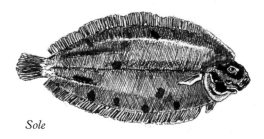

Sole

Method
Fillet the fish as previously described. Save all the trimmings and boil these gently for ten minutes in a little seasoned water to produce a fish stock. Poach the whole fish or the fillets in the strained fish stock in a fish kettle with a couple of slices of lemon for 8-10 minutes.

Serving
If you have poached the whole fish, now is the time to remove the dark skin and head prior to serving; a flat fish knife is the best implement to use. The white skin on the underside is much softer and most people don't bother to remove it prior to serving. Garnish with a little parsley and lemon slices, and serve in a 'green sea' of asparagus sauce.

Barbecued Sea Bass

Sea bass *(Dicentrarchus labrax)* are usually caught close inshore amongst the white foam of the breakers where they search for a meal churned up by the waves as they crash towards the beach. Not surprising then that these are muscular, powerful fish, and their solid white flesh is all the more tasty for it, with a robust flavour which will be well complemented by strong flavours and brought out by the high heat of a barbecue. This recipe combines the essential elements of good fish cooking, olive oil, lime juice and herbs. The herbs can be used to impart their flavours directly to the fish, and also be burnt on the barbecue to release their oils as a smoke to penetrate the flesh. Don't be sparing with the herbs, and while the use of Norfolk lavender as a culinary herb may not be common, in combination with rosemary it imparts a distinctive and delightful flavour to the flesh of the fish, and to its skin.

Ingredients
A whole fresh sea bass - about 2-3 lbs
Freshly picked rosemary, parsley, sage and lavender sprigs – 2 or 3 handfuls
Olive oil - about two thirds of a cupful
Lime and lemon juice - to make up to a cupful
Lemon/lime slices to garnish
Fresh vine leaves and twigs (if available)
Salt and freshly ground pepper

Lavender

Method
Gut and scale the fish if this hasn't already been done, being careful in handling it to avoid the sharp dorsal and pelvic spines, which should also be removed. Thoroughly wash the fish inside and out, and remove loose scales. Make four or five slash cuts diagonally across the fish on both sides. Pack these cuts, and also inside the fish with half the rosemary and lavender sprigs. Larger fish may be 'butterflied', i.e. the backbone removed and the fish gently flattened on a board to produces a shape which will cook more evenly and be easier to handle on the griddle. Mix the oil, juice and pepper and liberally brush the fish inside and out with this mixture. Do not add salt at this stage, it will toughen the flesh and make the fish too dry.

Barbecue
Prepare a generous fire using a mixture of charcoal and hardwood lit with paper. Don't be tempted to use firelighters or fluid, and avoid using pine or other softwood, as this will give a paraffin taste to the food – especially noticeable and disagreeable with the delicate flavour of fish. Allow to burn until most of the flame has died down, it will usually take about forty minutes, leaving a thick bed of grey glowing embers. Arrange the fire to the shape of the fish; flick the brush over the grill with oil to prevent sticking. Barbecuing relies on a fierce heat to sear and seal the flesh to retain juices; a cool fire will sweat out all the juices producing a tough dry result. Lay the fish on the grill, starting at the back so that each careful turning will move the fish to the front. Allow enough space for just three turns. A specially made fish griddle, obtainable from good cooking equipment shops, will make this job easier. A

fish slice should be used to ease the skin of the fish from the grill. Don't be tempted to turn the fish too soon; the longer you leave it the less sticking will occur as the skin carbonises where it touches the grill bars, but some sticking is inevitable. Cook for about fifteen minutes (depending on the size of the fish and the heat of the fire), brushing frequently with the oil mixture inside and out. Turn the fish and sear for another five to ten minutes. Add the vine twigs, leaves and woody parts of the rosemary and lavender to the coals to impart their distinctive smoky aromas to the fish. As the fire dies, allow another 5-10 minutes cooking time; arrange the embers to ensure that the thicker head end of the fish receives enough heat to produce a firm, juicy white flesh with a crisp, slightly charred skin.

Serving
Allow the fish to rest for a few minutes and then serve on a bed of vine leaves, garnish with lemon and lime wedges and sprinkle with a pinch of salt. Lubricate with one of the savoury butters described in Chapter 5. Serves 4-6.

Poached Whole Sea Bass

Take any ordinary piece of beef and poach it slowly in water with a bit of seasoning and the result will invariably be a tasty dish of meat and broth. Do the same with a piece of fish and the result will invariably be a disappointment of flabby fish with little flavour, albeit in a moderately tasty stock. Poaching fish in plain water simply doesn't work. You need to produce a court bouillon in which to cook the fish, ensuring that the flavour is retained within the fish and not lost. This recipe emphasises the wonderful flavour and richness of the meaty flesh of the bass. Small portions will prove quite adequate for the heartiest of appetites; a four-pound fish will easily serve 8 people.

Ingredients
Fresh sea bass about 3-4 pounds
Two sticks of celery
Button mushrooms
Fresh ground pepper & salt
Mixed herbs
Butter
Flour or corn flour
Lemon or lime slices to garnish
Watercress to garnish
White wine

Court Bouillon: Fish trimmings, onion, carrot, salt and pepper, bouquet garni

Preparation
Gut and scale the fish if this hasn't already been done, being careful in handling it to avoid the sharp dorsal and anal spines, which should also be removed. Thoroughly wash the fish inside and out; remove loose scales.

The fish will be poached in a court bouillon, which should be prepared in advance. Ensure that you have a large enough casserole dish to hold the fish comfortably. You may need to remove the head or tail, which may be used to prepare a fish stock as a basis for a sauce (see p. 128).

To prepare a court bouillon take a large sliced carrot, a chopped onion, bouquet garni and seasonings. Cover with water and simmer gently in a covered casserole dish for about an hour and a half, strain and allow to cool. Only the exceptionally lazy or wilfully deceitful host will use a fish stock cube, but we have all been there at one time or another! Certainly using a stock cube will be preferable to putting the fish into plain water.

Method

Place the whole fish in a large, covered casserole dish; add the court bouillon, the chopped celery, a few button mushrooms and a good splash of white wine. Sprinkle with mixed herbs and the salt and pepper. Place in a moderate oven for 20-30 minutes. Remove the fish and allow to rest. Thicken the pan juices with butter or single cream and a little flour or cornflour. Place on a large platter, pour over the pan juices and garnish with lemon, lime and watercress.

Serving

Serve with stir-fried vegetables, hot, crispy bread rolls, parsley butter and of course more white wine. Sufficient for 8-10 persons.

Rosamond's Sea Bass Farmhouse Casserole

Sea bass are muscular, powerful fish, and their solid white flesh in this robust recipe takes on a meaty texture akin to chicken. As the summer turns to autumn and the evenings draw in, this heartier treatment of the bass seems more appropriate. Unusually for a fish dish, this will withstand being kept hot for any late arrivals. The large bones of the fish are easily found and removed.

Ingredients

Sea bass 3-4 pounds (whole fish or steaks)
2 sticks of celery
Button mushrooms
Half-pound streaky bacon
Can of chopped tomatoes
2 large onions
Tablespoon of tomato purée
Freshly ground pepper
Salt
Basil
Mixed herbs
Butter
Bottle(s) of red wine

A fishing lugger of the Short Blue fleet

52

Preparation

Gut and scale the fish if this hasn't already been done, being careful in handling it to avoid the sharp dorsal and anal spines, which should be removed. Thoroughly wash the fish inside and out; remove loose scales. Cut the fish into portions that will easily fit into your microwave. If you have a whole fish, use the head and tail to make a fish stock for subsequent dishes.

Method

Make the casserole sauce by gently frying the bacon, onions and celery in butter until soft, sprinkle with the herbs, a little flour and seasonings. Place the sauce into a large, covered casserole dish; add the chopped mushrooms and tomatoes, a good splash of red wine and the tomato purée. Place in a pre-heated medium oven. Meanwhile, microwave the fish for about 5 minutes, long enough for the flesh to turn white which will make it easy to remove it from the skin and bones. Try to keep the fish in large chunks. Cook the sauce for about 20 minutes, and then add the chunks of fish. Finish for a further 10 minutes. Adjust the seasoning.

Serving

Serve with a mixture of long-grain and wild rice, your favourite salad and hot crusty bread, all accompanied with plenty of red wine. Sufficient for 6-8 persons.

Baked Sea Bass Parcel- A Dinner Party Speciality

The invention of aluminium foil has revolutionised fish cooking by allowing cooks to dispense with the need to poach the fish in a previously prepared court bouillon. The foil retains all the flavours and juices of the fish throughout the cooking process, particularly if the head is left on. This Jamie Oliver TV recipe is excellent for a dinner party since most of the work is in the preparation, undertaken long before the guests arrive. Having prepared the fish parcel, the cooking can continue unattended while the hosts entertain their guests, and the fish comes to the table bathed in its own sauce all ready for serving. The herbs and vegetables in the main dish are also used in the salad, but in different ways to give a wide range of flavours and textures. This method works equally well with grey mullet, which is similar, but invariably cheaper than sea bass.

Ingredients

A whole sea bass of 2-3 pounds (or grey mullet)
Head of fennel finely chopped
A large red onion finely chopped
Bunch of fresh basil roughly torn
3-4 bay leaves roughly torn
3 lemons
Tablespoon of olive oil
3 ounces butter
Coarse salt and coarse ground black pepper

Head of fennel

53

The Salad

Chop the celery into chunks and roughly tear the lettuce and some of the basil leaves into a bowl. Remove and keep the head of the fennel, slice the remainder together with the onion into fine slivers and mix with the lettuce and basil. Add pepper, salt, lemon juice and olive oil, turn gently to coat all the ingredients. Refrigerate until ready to serve.

The Fish Parcel

Gut, scale and clean the whole sea bass, make four-five shallow diagonal slashes on both flanks of the fish. Place the fish on a wide sheet of foil that is three times larger than the fish. Smooth the salt and pepper into the diagonal slashes, surround the fish with most of the chopped vegetables and herbs. Also pack the body cavity with most of the bay leaves, a knob of butter and some more vegetables. Drench the fish and vegetables with the olive oil and the juice of the lemons and dot freely with lumps of butter. Wrap the foil around the fish to form an airtight parcel by tightly folding the edges. Place on a shallow tray and bake in the oven for 8 minutes per pound in a moderate (220°C) oven.

Fennel Potatoes

Boil the scraped potatoes (new potatoes if available) in salted water until tender, turn into a sieve. Roughen the potatoes by shaking in the sieve; add a little olive oil, some pepper and the finely chopped head and leaves of the fennel. Finish with a squeeze of lemon juice.

The Bread

A good strongly flavoured wholemeal loaf; one that contains lots of soft grains or fruits is ideal for this dish. When you take the bass from the oven leave it to rest for 5 minutes while you put the bread into the oven to warm through prior to serving. Sea bass is very filling; a two-pound fish will easily serve 4 hungry people, a three-pound fish 6-8 persons. Grey mullet has a denser, less flaky texture than sea bass.

Baked Grey Mullet and Garlic Potatoes

A member of the perch family, the grey mullet, specifically the thick-lipped mullet (*Crenimugil labrosus*), is a summer visitor to our British shores, often preferring sheltered waters along rocky coasts or harbours. In these localities they feed on organic rich mud and scrape algae from rocks or harbour timbers using their specially designed fleshy-lipped mouths. Mullet may also be found in the lower reaches of rivers where they may be seen shoaling near the surface. The building of artificial rock reefs along the Norfolk coast has undoubtedly served to attract these fish to our beaches in greater numbers in the past few years. Although the feeding method of grey mullet is quite different from that of sea bass they are both powerful fish and in general appearance, colour and size-range they are quite similar; mullet are less well armoured and don't have the enormous head and gulping mouth of a sea bass. They also taste quite similar; the mullet has a denser, less flaky texture than the sea bass but is still just as meaty and filling. The main difference between the two is evident at the fishmonger's slab, where mullet is often half the price of the more popular sea bass. This recipe treats the fish quite simply with the well-tried mixture of oil and lemon to bring out flavour, combined with lots of parsley to add astringency, and then adds a dash of cream to make a magnificently smooth, flavour-packed sauce. Baking the onion and garlic reduces their pungency to a sweetness that will fill the kitchen with an irresistible aroma and impart a wonderful flavour to the humble potato for a memorable gastronomic experience.

Ingredients

Whole grey mullet (2-3 pounds)
One large lemon
Very large bunch of fresh parsley
Olive oil
Salt and pepper
Tablespoon of double cream
Peeled and quartered potatoes
Onion-quartered
Garlic cloves
Olive oil
Salt and pepper

Garlic

Garlic Potatoes

Placed the peeled and quartered potatoes, roughly chopped onion and finely chopped garlic cloves in a shallow dish. Drizzle with olive oil; season well with salt and pepper and stir well to coat everything with oil and seasoning. Place on the top shelf of a hot oven at least ten minutes prior to cooking the fish. Roast until golden brown.

Baked Grey Mullet

Snip off the fins with kitchen scissors, being careful to avoid the dorsal spines. Gut and scale the fish (the scales are particularly large and extend well onto the head) being sure to remove the thin, black lining of the cavity. If necessary remove the head and tail so that the fish will lie neatly on a trivet placed in a deep, lidded casserole. Wash the fish well and cut two or three diagonal slits across each flank. Brush with olive oil inside and out and season with salt and pepper. Lightly chop the parsley and slice half the lemon. Place slices of lemon and chopped parsley in the cavity, and also pack the cuts with chopped parsley. Place on the trivet in the pan, arrange lemon slices over and under the fish, drizzle with a little more olive oil. Squeeze the juice from the remaining half-lemon over the fish, and add a couple of tablespoons of water to the pan. Cover and place in a hot oven for around 30 minutes (allow 10 minutes per pound). For the last 10 minutes of cooking remove the casserole lid to braise the skin gently and reduce the stock. Remove the fish from the pan and allow to rest. Further reduce the stock and whisk in the double cream or thicken with a little flour and butter. Use the sauce, lemon slices and sprigs of parsley to garnish the fish.

Serve with the garlic potatoes, your favourite salad and, for the very hungry, hot, crusty bread. A two-pound fish will serve 4 people, a three-pounder 6 people.

Grey Mullet with Gooseberries

The coming of summer sees the arrival not only of grey mullet but also many other seasonal foods, including gooseberries. This recipe combines fish and fruit where the sweet and sour tartness of the gooseberries contrasts with the salty bacon to bring out the meaty flavour of the fish. When served with fresh asparagus and newly dug potatoes, this dish makes a summer treat without comparison. For an autumn variation substitute apples for the gooseberries and serve with baked potatoes.

Ingredients
2-3 pound whole grey mullet (or sea bass)
One pound of gooseberries
Large onion
3 sticks of celery
Parsley
Half a cup of wine vinegar or vintage cider
Fresh sage
3 rashers of bacon
Olive oil
Salt and pepper
Butter or single cream

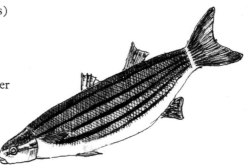

Grey Mullet

Method
Roughly chop the fruit, vegetables and herbs, mix well. Lightly coat the fish, inside and out with olive oil; place most of the fruit and vegetable mix in the cavity. Wrap the bacon rashers around the fish and hold in place with cocktail sticks. Season with salt and pepper. Place on a trivet in a large casserole dish, add the remainder of the vegetables, the cider vinegar and some more olive oil, and put the lid on. If you haven't got a large casserole you can use foil. Add the butter in dabs, double wrap the fish, seal well and place on a flat baking sheet. Place the casserole (or baking sheet) in a moderate oven for 20 minutes. If using a casserole remove the lid to reduce the liquid. Finish off for a further 5-10 minutes. Remove the fish and allow to rest, add the butter or cream to the pan and whisk to produce a lightly glazed sauce, or simply remove the foil being careful to retain the juices.

Serving
Serve the whole fish on a warmed plate, pour on the sauce and garnish with fresh parsley

Mullet and Bacon Kebabs

Mullet come to the Norfolk shores at the height of the barbecue season and these meaty fish are ideal for spearing onto kebab skewers and exposing to the fast heat of a barbecue. Only the most confident fisherman will actually light the barbecue before venturing down to the shore, but remember that a fish barbecue will only be successful if the grill is pre-heated to a high temperature before cooking begins. The well-prepared barbecuer will also have a herb garden planted within easy reach of the grill so that freshly-caught fish, freshly-picked herbs and summer sun combine to make a glorious alfresco meal. Bass or cod work equally well in this recipe.

Ingredients
2 pounds of grey mullet fillets
Olive oil
8 ounces of thick streaky bacon off-cuts (with the rind removed)
White wine vinegar (optional)
2 tablespoons of chopped sage leaves and a few whole leaves
Bay leaves
2 cloves of garlic
Salt and pepper
Lemon quarters
6 kebab skewers   *Sage*

Method
Scale, gut and clean the fish and remove two large fillets leaving the skin on. Cut the fish fillets into large enough cubes which will hold firmly onto the kebab skewers. Leaving the skin on will help in this respect. Place the chunks of fish in a bowl and drizzle on the olive oil and wine vinegar; set aside to marinade for a while. Crush the garlic and pound together with the finely chopped sage leaves; add salt and pepper, then add to the bowl and fold in with the fish. Cut the bacon into one-inch squares and thread onto the kebab skewers alternating bacon with the cubes of mullet, slot a couple of sage and bay leaves between the pieces of meat. Using bacon off-cuts often means that you get lumps of bacon fat which you can flatten into discs and thread these onto the skewers where they will serve to baste the rest of the meat. Rub the oil and herb mixture into the kebabs, and continue to baste them with the mixture as you grill them for around 15 minutes. At the same time give each kebab a good squeeze of lemon juice so that they stay nice and moist. A couple of strategically-placed bricks on either side of barbecue will allow you to 'spit roast' the kebabs without actually resting them on the grill, thus avoiding any sticking. Turn every couple of minutes until the bacon has crisped and the fish has set to a white opaqueness with slightly browned edges. If you don't want to overdo the garlic, just give the kebabs a bit of a tingle by spearing each skewer up to the hilt and back through a clove of garlic and leave it at that.

Serving
Serve on a bed of salad leaves garnished with fresh herbs. Serves 6.

Herb Crusted Mixed Grill

This recipe uses fish steaks, which are simply prepared by taking the scaled and gutted fish and cutting through the main body to produce three or four 1½ inch (40mm) thick portions. Put the fish on a cutting board and use a heavy knife to cut around the flesh and remove the head. Sever the backbone by chopping down on the back of the knife with your heel of your hand. Allow about five inches (13cm) at the tail end to make a decent steak, remove the tail fin by the same chopping method. The fish steaks can be cooked on the barbecue, grilled or baked in the oven; whichever method is chosen the essence of this recipe is to sear the fish quite quickly under a high heat. The protective herb coat will ensure that the flesh of the fish does not dry out, whilst the skin will become deliciously crispy taking on the intense flavours of the herbs. The combination of the meaty white flesh of the sea bass, the moister and softer texture of the grey mullet and the rich intensity of the oilier pink flesh of the salmon trout *(Salmo trutto)* provides an exceptional mixture of texture and flavours, a mixed grill to remember!

Ingredients
Thick steaks of sea bass, salmon trout and grey mullet
Olive oil
Butter
Salt
Herb seasoning:
Level tablespoon crushed pink peppercorns
Level tablespoon dried onion powder
Teaspoon garlic salt
2 heaped tablespoons dried tarragon
2 heaped tablespoons dried dill
2 teaspoons of grated and dried lemon peel
Teaspoon of paprika
Teaspoon milled black pepper

Garnish
A dozen mussels in their shells, well scrubbed
Salad leaves
Parsley

Tarragon

Method
Prepare the herbs and seasonings in advance by simply mixing the crushed or grated dried ingredients. Store in a sealed container to allow the flavours to mingle. These days there are any number of good traditional herb suppliers who will be able to provide a ready-mixed seasoning of a similar composition to the above; look out for them at country fare and food shows. Lightly coat the steaks of fish in olive oil and press firmly into the seasoning mixture to ensure an even coating. Avoid salting the fish at this stage, as this will dry it out. Grill or barbecue for 5-8 minutes on each side over a high heat; alternatively bake in a hot oven for 20 minutes. Allow the fish

to rest for 5 minutes. In the meantime put the mussels on the grill where they will happily bubble and cook in their own juices for 2-3 minutes. Gently heat the butter in a saucepan and skim the surface to clarify, stir in a generous sprinkling of the herb mixture.

Serving

Lightly salt the fish before placing on a bed of salad leaves lining a large platter. Surround with the gaping mussels and pour over the herb butter. Trim with parsley and any other salad ingredients, and take to the table.

Sea Trout

Sea trout *(Salmo trutto)* are the same species as river trout but they have a coastal marine life-cycle, only taking to fresh water in order to breed. As their other common name, 'salmon trout', suggests, they are very similar to salmon *(Salmo salar)* and it takes someone with a good working knowledge of the two fish to tell them apart. Both salmon and sea trout have dark, round and X-shaped spots on their bellies, in the salmon these are confined to the area above the lateral line, in the sea trout some also occur below, and there are usually a few red spots as well. Another difference is in the shape of these fish just in front of the tail, an area called the 'caudal peduncle'. In the salmon it is comparatively thinner making a good firm handhold, but in the sea trout it is much thicker. So, if you grab your lifeless salmon by the tail and it still slips through your fingers it's actually a sea trout! Both species have a distinctive fleshy adipose fin located near the tail that can give an indication of the age of the fish; a ragged adipose fin indicates an older specimen. Any salmon with blunt fins is almost certainly a farmed specimen that has worn them smooth by constantly buffeting into the sides of its cage. However, when it comes to taste, the sea trout is incomparably better, given that so much of the salmon we eat today is farmed fish with a colour and texture resembling bright pink blotting paper. Not so the sea trout; the flesh comes in firm meaty flakes with a delicate blush of pink, and by mid summer the high oil content of the fish gives it a taste that is out of this world. Since the oil is of healthy, unsaturated fat, the sea trout is truly a king of fish. Sadly, you will be hard pushed to find a fishmonger on the east coast who can supply wild sea trout and even if he can the high price may push you towards the supermarket's counter and farmed fare. Incidentally, beware the term 'catch of the day': my local supermarket advertises salmon and sea trout special offers in this way, but close inspection of the label, with only a small magnifying glass, reveals that the fish on offer is actually a farmed specimen. In the face of such obvious deceit what, or who, is the catch of the day I wonder? Go to the Welsh coast on the other hand and ask for *sewin* and you will be sure to be served with wild sea trout at an affordable price, for here the wide estuaries provide a steady supply. Because it is so tasty, the sea trout doesn't take much to reveal its true colours. Fillets pan-fried in butter (there goes the healthy eating!) are quite superb. Poached as a whole fish in a court bouillon in the same way as salmon, it will eat brilliantly hot or cold, and given all the trimmings it will always make a fine centrepiece for the table. This recipe is also for a whole fish, but it keeps things simple and lets the flavour of the fish shine through.

Baked Sea Trout with Fennel *(see front cover)*

Ingredients
Whole sea trout (2-3 pounds)
Fennel fronds
Butter
Salt and pepper

Béchamel sauce   *Fennel*

Preparation
Gut the fish, removing the fins, but since the scales are small and thin, it is usually not worth bothering to remove them. Remove the head if the whole fish is too big to go in your pan. Gently simmer the head with a carrot, small onion and bouquet garni to make a fish stock for the accompanying sauce.

Method
Lightly smear the body cavity with the butter and pack with the fennel fronds. Lightly butter the outside of the fish; season with salt and pepper and place on a greased baking tray. Cover with foil and bake in a moderate heat for 5 minutes per pound plus another 5 minutes with the foil removed to finish off. Allow to rest for 5 minutes before serving.

Serving
Can be served hot or cold with simply boiled potatoes and summer vegetables or salad, all moistened with a simple white or béchamel sauce (see p. 132). Sea trout is rich and 6 people will do well to finish a three-pounder; any leftovers can be mixed with a scant dollop of mayo to make some very superior sandwiches for lunch the next day, or adapted to the following recipe for a mouth-watering mousse.

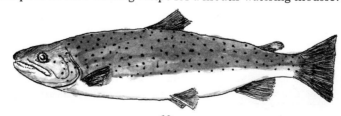

Sea Trout

Fresh Sea Trout Mousse

Ingredients
One pound of fresh sea trout or salmon fillet
Small carton of double cream
4 large egg whites
One tablespoon lemon juice
One tablespoon of fresh dill (chopped finely)
One ounce of butter

Alternative
Pieces of chopped smoked sea trout
Canapé rounds

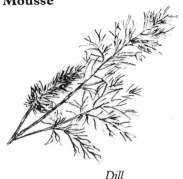

Dill

Method
Lightly butter eight ramekin dishes. Remove the skin from the fish (use with any other trimmings to produce stock or as a crispy starter, see below). Cut the fish into chunks, season with salt, pepper, nutmeg and lemon juice. Place all this in a food processor and reduce to a fine purée. Add the double cream and whiz again. Remove the bowl and fold in the egg whites and sprinkle in the chopped dill. Spoon the mixture into the ramekins and refrigerate until ready to cook. Place the ramekin dishes into a roasting tin and pour in enough hot water to come half way up the sides of the dishes. Bake in a moderate (170°C/340°F) pre-heated oven until set, about 15-20 minutes.

Serving
Unmould onto warm plates in a sea of your chosen sauce (asparagus perhaps, see Chapter 5) and serve with toast. Alternatively, mix in pieces of chopped, smoked sea trout and serve as canapés on small rounds of toast or pastry. Sufficient for 8 as a starter or canapés.

Salt-Cured Sea Trout

The Scandinavians cold cure their salmon or sea trout in a mixture of salt, herbs and sugar with a strong emphasis on the aniseed flavour of dill. They call it *gravad lax*, meaning 'buried salmon', for in times past the dish was buried in the frozen soil to cure. Now that we are blessed with refrigerators the process is far simpler and undoubtedly more hygienic. This recipe uses a similar technique and is closely related to *gravad lax* but comes from the southern climate of the Mediterranean, which explains the hotter blend of spices and garlic accompaniment.

Ingredients
2 sea trout or salmon fillets
2 tablespoons of salt
2 tablespoons of Demerara sugar
One teaspoon of chilli powder

One teaspoon milled black pepper
3 tablespoons of freshly chopped coriander
Parsley garnish

Method

Cut the fillets into thick, flat slices which will neatly fit into a shallow dish. Mix in a bowl the salt, sugar, chilli powder, pepper and coriander and then rub this mixture into the flesh of each fish portion. Place a layer of pieces in the dish skin-side down; place another layer on top skin-side up, then cover everything with foil and place a weight on the top. Refrigerate for at least two days, turning the fillets every now and then to allow them to baste evenly in the liquid pickle, which will soon form. Drain the pieces and pat dry, transfer to a board and slice diagonally from the skin into wafer-thin slices.

Serving

Serve chilled with a dollop of aioli garlic mayonnaise (see p. 135) and garnish with the parsley and the deep-fried skin of the fish (see next recipe).

Parsley

Sea Trout Skin

I recently saw one of those TV lifestyle programmes where a trendy designer extolled the virtues of 'salmon leather' as a new home furnishing concept; evidently the dried and cured skins are sold as a by-product of the Canadian canning industry. However, the Spanish stick to a purely culinary use for this normally discarded by-product and use it as a *tapas* dish, (a *tapas* spread comprises a wide range of tasty bites, often served on the bar counter) or as a crispy garnish to other fish dishes.

Ingredients
Sea trout or salmon skin
Salt
Oil for frying

Method
Scrape any remaining flesh from the skin and cut into half-inch (12½mm) wide strips. Drop into hot oil and fry for about a minute until curled, brown and crisp. Drain on kitchen paper and lightly salt.

Serving
Serve immediately with a favourite dip.

Sea Trout and Herb Tart

This herb-laden tart has an ancient pedigree dating from medieval times when fish tarts were an essential part of the diet for 'fish days', when the Church stipulated that meat should not be eaten, though this rich dish was only for those that could afford such fine fare. Fruits and spices were often included with the main ingredient, but this recipe uses mostly herbs and a couple of spices, the type and quantities suggested being intended to act merely as a guide for the adventurous cook. Salmon works just as well as sea trout in this tart; try mixing fresh and smoked fish for further variety.

Ingredients

8 ounces of plain shortcrust pastry
One and a half pounds of sea trout or salmon fillets
3 tablespoons of chopped fresh parsley and some sprigs for garnish
3 tablespoons of chopped fresh tarragon
2 ounces of butter
2 tablespoons of olive oil
2 garlic cloves, chopped finely
Juice of one lemon
Quarter of a teaspoon of grated nutmeg
Quarter of a teaspoon of ground cinnamon
Salt and Freshly-ground black pepper
2 eggs and 2 egg yolks
Half pint of double cream

Tarragon

Method

Line a deep nine-inch tin with the pastry; add a sheet of baking foil and cover with baking beans. Bake blind for 15 minutes at 200°C; remove the baking sheet and beans and prick the pastry base all over with a fork. Brush with a little beaten egg; return to the oven and bake for a further 5-10 minutes until it turns a golden brown; remove and allow to cool. In the meantime, proceed to cook the fish by chopping it into chunks, ensuring that any bones are removed. Mix the fish with the herbs in a large bowl to making sure that each piece of fish receives an even, green coating. Heat the oil and butter in a heavy-bottomed pan and fry the garlic for a scant minute, then add the coated fish chunks. Fry them quickly to seal the juices (the herb coat will prevent them being overcooked), and add the spices and lemon juice. Season with salt and pepper, give them a quick stir, then transfer to the pastry case. Use the same bowl to blend the leftover herbs, eggs, egg yolks and cream. Adjust the seasoning and then pour into the pastry case. Adjust the pre-heated oven to 190°C and bake for 35-40 minutes until the mixture has set; keep warm for serving.

Serving

Serve as a hot dish with new potatoes or plain boiled rice and green vegetables, accompanied by a simple white sauce. Alternatively, serve cold with a rice based summer salad.

63

Barbecued Mackerel (or Herring) with Gooseberry Sauce

Mackerel is an oily fish where the oil is distributed throughout the flesh of the creature, unlike white fish where their oil content is generally confined to their internal organs, principally the liver. Fish need this oil as an essential part of their physiology given their watery habitat. However, this means that when you apply heat to fish like mackerel and herring, the oil is driven off in the form of a fine aerosol, which produces a highly distinctive and lingering smell. For this reason both species have gained a certain notoriety and many people are reluctant to have them in the house, despite their tastiness on the plate. The answer is simply to cook them on the barbecue, and the arrival of the mackerel in high summer makes this eminently possible. While it is a happy accident of nature that mackerel and gooseberries appear in Norfolk at the same time of year, it was no accident that a clever cook decided to combine them on the plate; the tartness of the fruit superbly complements the oiliness of the fish. The modest price of mackerel means that you can indulge all of your friends, while filling the garden with a heady aroma, invoking happy memories of Mediterranean holidays and southern beaches. Indeed, the French name for gooseberries is *groseilles a maquereau,* mackerel berries.

Ingredients
A dozen fresh mackerel, horse mackerel or herring
Olive oil
Lemon juice
Gooseberry sauce (see p. 136)

Method
Gut the fish, snip off the fins and tails, leaving the heads on, (the oil in the head bastes the fish during cooking and greatly adds to the flavour). Wash thoroughly; slash the sides of the fish to prevent curling and to allow the marinade to penetrate the flesh. Make up the oil and lemon juice mixture and let the fish marinade in a shallow dish while you build a hot fire using paper, sticks and charcoal (never use firelighters). Once the coals have turned to an intense hot grey ash (it usually takes about half an hour) lay the fish on the grill and continue to baste at regular intervals with the marinade. Avoid turning for as long as possible, you need to leave the fish long enough to carbonise the flesh, once this happens you will be able to turn them without too much sticking. Cook the fish for a good 10 minutes until the skin is crisped and showing brown at the edges. Have the gooseberry sauce warming on one side.

Herring Alternative
If using herring, flatten the gutted fish by placing it on a board and pressing firmly along its back, turn over and tease out the backbone. In the same way as kippers cook them in pairs placed flesh to flesh with a dab of butter, twist of pepper and a squeeze of lemon as the 'sandwich filling'. Cooking them in this way means that when you turn the sandwich the oils from one fillet baste the other to give

superlative flavour, but remember to put the fish in a barbecue griddle to facilitate this turning.

Serving
Serve on a bed of lettuce garnished with the gooseberry sauce. Provide salt for those who want it, if you add it sooner it will harden the flesh of the fish. Add your favourite side salad and crusty bread. Eat immediately, serves 6.

The Cartilaginous Fishes – Skate and Dogfish

Scientists divide the world of fishes into two categories, bony fish and cartilaginous fish. Skate fall into the latter group, which not only explains their distinctive flavour and texture, but also why their 'bones', which are really cartilage, are soft enough to eat. Unlike bony fish, which rapidly decompose in summer weather, freshly caught skate needs to be hung like a piece of game for the flesh to develop its full flavour and suitable texture. If the fish hasn't been gutted (a very messy business, preferably done at sea to dispose of the offal more easily) this should be done prior to hanging the fish, head-down, in a shady spot or cool outhouse. Two days is usually enough to achieve the desired effect, but in very sultry weather reduce this to overnight. Fillet the fish by cutting off each wing following the natural line of the body; on larger specimens plenty of solid flesh will be found in the middle section, while underneath the fish you will find two large balls of meat rather like the 'oysters' found on the back of a chicken. Remove the dark skin (a pair of pliers may prove useful) and cut off the tips of the spiny thorns that give this fish its alternative name of 'thornback' *(Raja clavata)*. You will find that the rest of the thorn resembles a hard, white, striated 'Mint Imperial', embedded in the flesh of the fish, but these can easily be removed when on the plate. Through the 1950s and 60s skate could be caught off Norfolk beaches with a rod and line, but those days are long gone and nowadays the fish is usually netted well offshore. I need a good, calm, August day to consider venturing the couple of miles offshore to reach the likely haunts of the skate in my small boat.

Skate

65

Dogfish (Rock Salmon)

Dogfish can be caught from the beach but, like skate, they are becoming less common close inshore; tangle netting is the preferred method of catching them. There are a number of different species of dogfish found in Norfolk waters, the lesser spotted *(Scyliorhinus caniculus),* the greater-spotted or nursehound *(Scyliorhinus stellaris),* the spurdog *(Squalus acanthias)* and the smoothhound or 'smoothie' *(Mustelus mustelus).* These are all members of the shark family and like skate they are all cartilaginous. When prepared for the table, dogfish are given a variety of local names which include huss, rock salmon or even catfish. Norfolk fishermen named them 'sweet Williams', an ironic term stemming from the less than pleasant smell experienced when they are gutted. If you can stick the smell, gutting them is pretty straightforward, but when it comes to removing the skin, be prepared for a struggle! Most people know that sharkskin, unlike the skin of bony fish, does not have a covering of scales; instead the scales or denticles are contained within the skin, making it very rough, and very tough. In the past it has been used as sandpaper and as decorative 'shagreen,' a form of green mottled leather. However, what most people don't know is that it is extremely well attached to the fish and stoutly resists any attempt to remove it.

Skinning Dogfish

Arm yourself with a knife, a hammer, a good-sized nail, a pair of pliers, some coarse salt and a rough wooden board. A friend with a firm grip may be needed as well. Hammer the nail through the head of the fish lying face down on the board, or fix one end of a small butcher's hook over the edge of the board while the other is speared through the throat of the fish to hold it firm. Remove the fins and tail and remove the long thin belly-flaps. This seems like a waste but if you leave them on they will hamper you in making the long, straight pull required to complete the skinning process. (The Germans smoke the belly into a popular snack, traditionally sold in the many fish stalls found in every seaside town.) Cut around the neck and, with salty fingers and the knife edge, ease up enough skin all round to give you a good grip with the pliers, and then pull towards the tail with a steady motion. You may need the friend to hang on to the head, the board or any bit that moves! Chop the fish into portions, leaving the backbone in the fish. Good luck!

Lesser Spotted Dogfish

Grilled Skate

The classic restaurant method of serving skate is to grill it garnished with capers and black butter sauce. Combining heated butter with vinegar produces the black butter. I suspect that this technique was adopted by restaurateurs as a means of ensuring that any slight ammonia taint, to which even the freshest piece of skate may be prone, is effectively masked. However, in your own kitchen such precautions should not be necessary, just cooking the fish will normally ensure that any such taint will be lost.

Ingredients
2 fresh wings of skate
Butter
Parsley
Salt and pepper

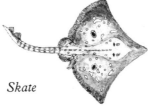

Skate

Method
My family all agree that the best method for skate is to grill it under a high heat for five minutes per side with the addition of a knob or two of plain butter and a light seasoning of pepper.

Serving
Add a little salt as preferred, serve with buttered new potatoes, a sprinkling of chopped parsley and one of the savoury butters described in Chapter 5. Serves 2.

Oriental Baked Rock Salmon

Dogfish has a very soft texture and is invariably given no other treatment than deep-frying in batter where it is sold under the name of 'rock salmon'. Much of the dogfish caught off Norfolk goes to fish and chip shops, particularly to the London area, where the sweet taste seems to be particularly relished. This dish with its strong spices provides a classic, oriental, sweet and sour dimension to the fish, while the salt and lemon juice marinade serves to firm up the texture and immeasurably improves the flavour.

Ingredients
4 large skinned rock salmon fillets
Clove of garlic
Lemon and/or lime juice
Bunch of chopped coriander leaves
Onion
Green chilli finely chopped (leave in the seeds for a very spicy dish)
4 tablespoons of olive oil
Salt and pepper

Method

Place the fish in a shallow ovenproof dish; season well with salt and pepper. Mix one tablespoon of olive oil with the lemon and lime juice and marinade the fish for an hour in the fridge, turning once or twice. When you are ready to start cooking, gently fry the garlic, onion and chilli in the rest of the olive oil to release and mix the flavours. Remove the fish from the fridge and pour on the spicy oil; sprinkle with the coriander and add a dash more olive oil. Bake uncovered in a moderate oven for around 20 minutes until the fish shows opaque white with just a hint of browning.

Serving

Serve immediately on a bed of wild rice garnished with lemon wedges, finely chopped coriander and Maitre d'hotel butter. Serves 4.

Shrimping

One of the joys of the Norfolk coast in high summer is a traditional shrimp tea, and if that tea comprises brown shrimps *(Crangon crangon)* that you have caught yourself, the delight is multiplied a hundredfold. Add the fact that the energy you expend in catching them will ensure a hearty appetite, and the whole process is guaranteed to provide a memorable experience.

The best time for catching shrimps by hand, using a push net, is in high summer at the lowest spring tides that occur every fortnight in the days immediately following the new or full moon. The good Lord, in His wisdom, has arranged that, along the Norfolk coast from Cromer down to Great Yarmouth, these low spring tides invariably occur during the early to mid afternoon, which gives the ardent shrimper every opportunity to gather the catch and get it home in good time for high tea. You can catch shrimps in winter; indeed one of the best catches I ever made was in early November, when all I needed was a bucket to scoop them out of the water. However, such bounty is very rare, and for winter shrimping you will need a wetsuit to cope with immersion in cold water for long periods. Don't even think of going shrimping at high tide; you won't catch anything and you may put yourself in danger by venturing out of your depth. Strong currents can sweep you off your feet, especially when hampered by an unwieldy shrimp net. On some east coast beaches the retreating tide leaves long shallow pools ('lows' in Norfolk dialect) on the beach and these may be full of shrimps, it's always worth trying these first before venturing into 'the main'.

Catching shrimps involves plodding along in waist-deep water, pushing the net in front of you and occasionally returning to the shore to empty it. Rather than a push net, some people prefer to use a smaller version of a trawl net, which is dragged through the shallows by a rope over the shoulder. On the northern French coast the locals employ a similar system but get well trained ponies to do all the hard work. Trawl shrimping, whether by hand or from a shallow draft boat, is usually carried out in the same direction as the tidal flow to increase the chances of catching flat fish, which always swim against, rather than with the prevailing current.

Having made your run, the net will, with luck, contain a shimmering orb of molten glass; these are brown shrimps, which in life are a transparent grey and will only turn the pinky brown colour that gives them their name when cooked. Turn them out onto a sheet of plastic spread on the sand and weighted down with stones to keep as much sand off them as possible. This will save you extra rinsing as well as preventing you from filling the waste trap of the sink with sand. Pick out the biggest and put them in a wicker basket, protecting them from the full sun with a piece of seaweed; local tradition has it that keeping them in a pail of seawater will drown them! In emptying your net you should discard and carefully return to the sea the undersized shrimps and the seaweed, crabs, starfish, cuttlefish and other sea creatures which you will also have collected; here you must be careful.

For be warned, you are not the only one who likes shrimps! One of their greatest predators is the lesser weever *(Trachinus vipera)*, a small silver and black fish with a distinctive yellow mark on the tail, and an even more distinctive set of black barbs on its back and gill covers. The barbs contain a poison that gives the weever its common name, the stinging fish, and the sting of a weever is a painful experience. (As the Latin name suggests weever comes from the Old French *wivre*, meaning a viper). If you do get stung you will be well advised to seek medical aid, for the venom is a powerful nerve poison containing a chemical that causes intense pain. However, the poison is destroyed by heat, so putting the affected part in very hot water can help to break down the venom and alleviate the pain; the increased blood flow caused by the

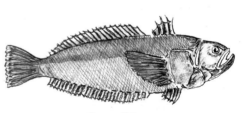

Lesser Weever

heat also assists natural cleaning and healing. The sting will not cause permanent damage but prevention is better than cure, so shore shrimpers should always wear sand shoes to protect their feet. Other precautions include fitting a small piece of line and a toggle on the bag end of the shrimp net to help shake the shrimps out, and using an old fork rather than fingers to sort the catch and spot any weevers. You will be able to catch shrimps through the afternoon until the tide starts to turn, for as soon as this happens the shrimps, knowing that bigger fish will soon be gliding across the deepening shallows, will bury themselves deeper in the sand and you will catch no more.

A Traditional Shrimp Tea

Having collected a basket full of shrimps, (five or six pints on a good day is quite possible) the dedicated gourmet will also take home a bucket of sea-water to cook them in, but most will agree that this is taking things just a bit too far! If some of the shrimps look slightly different to the rest and have red/golden eyes on stalks you will probably have caught some prawns, *(Palaeomeanas serratus)*; look for the long prong of its saw-toothed rostrum on the forehead. Cooking the shrimps is simple; peeling them takes longer, so be prepared. The steamy aroma of cooking shrimps will announce to the world that summer is here and all and sundry will be drawn to your kitchen with appetites sharpened by sea, sun and sand. Given a little training, even the most ham-fisted will soon be peeling shrimps like a veteran, so you need only provide a stack of buttered bread and a large pot of tea and let them get on with it.

Ingredients
Brown shrimps
4-6 tablespoons of salt
Water
Watercress
Bread and butter
Pepper
Lemon quarters

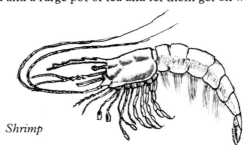

Shrimp

Method
Batch cook the shrimps in a solid-based pan with a lid; the idea is to retain as much heat as possible. Put about half an inch (12½mm) of water in the pan together with the salt and bring to a good rolling boil. (Too much water will make it difficult to maintain the pan at boiling point resulting in over-softened shrimps that will taste soggy and be difficult to peel.) Sort through the shrimps (which should still be alive and jumping) discarding any bits of seaweed and debris; give them a quick rinse under a running tap in a colander to remove any sand. Place about a pint of shrimps (three good handfuls) into the boiling water, put the lid on, and once the water has returned to the boil (in about a minute) the shrimps will be cooked and display their distinctive brown colour. Remove with a draining spoon and place in a colander to drain and cool; repeat the process until all are cooked.

Serving
Peel the shrimps, (everyone has their own technique), providing a bowl for all the tails and heads. which you may well wish to keep (see Crab or Lobster Bisque on p. 20). My technique for peeling involves taking the head and tail of the shrimp in each hand and breaking its back, pulling off the tail shell to reveal half of the body, and then taking hold of this part and gently teasing it from the head part of the shell. I am then left with a soft, moist, brownish-pink curl of succulence that only needs a hint of lemon juice and a drop of pepper before arranging with a few others on a thickly buttered slice of brown bread. A couple of handfuls of watercress and a pot of strong tea complete the picture.

Dabs, Plaice and Flounders

Dabs *(Limanda limanda)* are highly underrated, small, sandy-coloured flatfish, relatives of the sole, and distinguishable from flounders *(Platicthys flesus)* by an arch in the lateral line behind the left eye. Flounders are close cousins of the plaice *(Pleuronectes platessa);* both species have rusty spots, but in the flounder they are much less distinctive, neither do they have the bony nodules on the head which distinguish the plaice. Incidentally, lemon sole *(Microstomus kitt)* is another close relative, indeed far closer to the dab (the French name is *Limande-sole)* than its better-tasting namesake the Dover sole *(Solea solea).* Lemon soles are not common off the Norfolk coast but all the other species mentioned breed in shallow water and may frequently be caught close inshore. When they get older, plaice migrate to deeper offshore waters, whilst flounders will travel many miles up our local rivers and are frequently taken by coarse anglers trying their luck on the riverside in Norwich. Flounders make this journey in the summer in search of food, but at the first frosts they will head back towards the sea and over-winter in the tidal mud of Breydon Water. In times past flounders would often fall foul of the Breydon wildfowlers, who would take to their gun-punts and go 'butt darting' to supplement their meagre existence with some fresh fish. Butt is the Norfolk name for a flounder (from *but*, the Dutch word for flounder, perhaps, says the *Oxford English Dictionary*, 'from the blunt shape of the head') and is yet another example of how the people of the Low Countries have influenced our Norfolk language. The darts were barbed tridents mounted on long poles used to spear the fish as they lay in the mud; the men soon came to know the spots where the fish would usually bury themselves. If they avoid the butt darters, come the spring, the call of nature will see the flounders heading back to the open sea to breed. Flounders are less tasty than dabs or plaice and the flesh tends to be more watery, (some say like boiled cotton wool!) but they are enormously improved by adding the shrimps in this recipe.

Rosamond's Dabs Stuffed with Shrimps

A good afternoon's shrimping can produce a gallon or more of shrimps, enough to see off the heartiest of appetites leaving some for this recipe. A lucky shrimper may also net a flatfish, but whether caught yourself or purchased from the fishmonger this dish combines both for a fish supper that will tempt anyone (although my fishing partner, Derek, swears that the 'best ever' breakfast is a plate of fried dabs *(Limanda limanda)* caught on the previous evening's slack tide and matured overnight in the fridge).

71

Flatfish

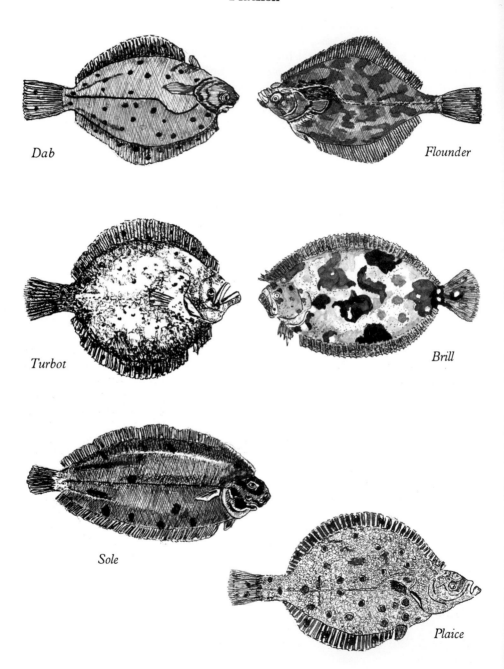

Dab

Flounder

Turbot

Brill

Sole

Plaice

Ingredients
8-10 dabs, flounders or plaice (about 2½pounds of fish)
One pint of boiled and peeled shrimps
Flour
Salt and pepper
Butter

Method
Gut the fish, remove the heads and make two cuts in the flesh parallel to the backbone forming two pockets. Coat the fish in flour and stuff the pockets with the shrimps. Place on a greased baking tray, add dabs of butter and season each fish. Bake in a medium hot oven for about 20 minutes, or gently shallow fry if preferred.

Serving
Served on a large platter garnished with lemon, boiled egg salad and chopped parsley, this dish looks quite splendid with a 'shoal' of fish swimming in a sea of parsley, their delicate white flesh peeking through the crown of shrimps. Serve with freshly baked bread rolls. Serves 3-4.

Plaice Chowder

In netting for bass and mullet I invariably catch a lot of modest-sized plaice, too small to fillet but too big to be thrown back. (Unlike round fish such as bass or mullet, flatfish survive perfectly well when trapped in a tangle net and the tiddlers swim off quite happily if carefully removed from the meshes.) So I keep the bigger specimens and simply make a V-shaped cut to remove the head, draw out the guts, chop off the tail and fins and store them in bags in the freezer. Battered and deep-fried as plaice on the bone, they make a tasty alternative to fish and chip shop fare; even then I still have plenty left for other purposes. Some go into the smokehouse, I use them up (fresh and smoked) in Lobster Bisque and also in this fish chowder. Chowder is a stew of fish and potatoes that got its name from the Atlantic seabord of France where Breton fishermen used a *chaudière*, a large iron cauldron, to cook their simple 'one-pot' dishes, either on board or over a driftwood fire on the beach. The word got anglicised to chowder when the dish travelled to America with the whaling industry (the whale's blubber was also rendered down in an enormous *chaudière*). Adding some local spices and shellfish, coast-dwellers from New England to Louisiana have claimed the dish for their own as Clam Chowder. This seaman's recipe combines fish and meat in a stew that, with its rough and ready character and strong flavours, allows ample scope for experimentation; try adding other vegetables such as sweet corn, peppers or roots, season the flour with a little curry powder or replace the white wine with a strong red.

Ingredients
4 pounds of small flatfish, plaice, sole, flounder, dabs (fresh and/or smoked)
Half a pound of cubed smoked bacon, or even better, smoked belly pork
Seasoned flour

6 onions roughly chopped into quarters
One large clove of garlic
Bouquet garni and bay leaves
Half a pound of mushrooms (roughly chopped or button)
4 ounces of butter
One pound of small whole potatoes, well scrubbed
Half a bottle of white wine diluted with as much water.
Single cream
Salt and pepper

Method

Gut and clean the fish removing the head, tail and fins (be generous so as to remove all those annoying lateral pin bones) but don't remove the skin. Gently fry the cubed and lightly floured bacon or belly pork in a dab of butter with a little finely sliced onion. Meanwhile, arrange the rest of the onions, garlic and bouquet garni in the bottom of a large fireproof pot, salt well, dot with some butter and throw in half a dozen peppercorns. Cover with the whole, unpeeled potatoes, add the bacon and arrange the cleaned fish on top, dotting with the rest of the butter. Cover with the diluted wine and bring to the boil, simmering for half an hour or longer until the potatoes are cooked. Keep an eye on the fish and remove to a warming oven when just cooked, and then remove the potatoes. Reduce by half the remaining liquid by boiling down and adjust the seasoning.

Serving

Return the fish and potatoes to the pot, take to the table and serve immediately into deep dishes also providing soupspoons and chunks of bread for your guests to mop up the delicious gravy. A bone plate will also be useful. Serves 8.

Leftovers make hearty soup. Remove the fish from the bone; finely dice any remaining bacon and potatoes; return to the gravy and carefully reheat.

Brill and Turbot

Brill *(Scophtalmus shombus)* and its close relative the turbot *(Psetta maxima)* are classified as flatfish like the humble plaice, dab or flounder, but these two fish, with their firm, white flesh, are widely regarded as the choicest pickings from the fishmonger's slab. Traditionally turbot has been given the crown, but either fish, freshly cooked, eat wonderfully; catching one of them in my net will bring a slow grin of satisfaction in anticipation of the delight to come. Not surprisingly they are expensive fish, brill usually being slightly cheaper than turbot. In distinguishing the two, brill is a little more oval in outline than the dinner-plate shape of turbot, which has bony bumps on its back. These bumps give the turbot its name; *tur* - means thorny whilst -*bot* is a corruption of *butt,* a flounder. Both fish have a white underbelly and a camouflaged and speckled dorsal surface that changes hue to match its surroundings. They spend the winter in deeper North Sea waters but come inshore to shallow water in the early summer to spawn. I only catch them later in the season when there has been a fair spell of calm, hot weather, and then only rarely. If you have a large enough circular fish kettle (all the best stately homes have enormous copper ones hanging in their kitchens) you can poach whole turbot or brill in a *court bouillon* and serve with new potatoes and summer vegetables, with the poaching liquor zipped up with double cream or whisked butter. Such simple treatment works well and of course looks magnificent when brought to the table, but fillets of the fish taste just as good. The essential element of these fish is the intensity of the whiteness of their flesh and this recipe uses the creams and beige of mushrooms in a sauce to emphasise and offset this whiteness, whilst the delicate flavours of the fungi do nothing to detract from the sweetness of the fish itself.

Roasted Turbot with Mushroom Sauce

Ingredients
Skinned turbot fillets
Oil
Salt and pepper
Mushroom sauce

Method
Pre-heat a lightly oiled heavy-base pan until it is just about glowing, and while you are waiting start the mushroom sauce (see p. 138). Lightly brush each side of the fillets with a little more oil and place the fillets in the pan for about three minutes, resisting the temptation to poke them about. Carefully turn once, reduce the heat and cook for a scant couple of minutes more.

Serving
Place on warmed plates and keep warm while you quickly finish the sauce, (or zap the prepared sauce in the microwave), marry the two together and eat immediately.

Oysters

You will find Pacific oysters *(Ostrea gigas)* being grown commercially and harvested around the Brancaster and Thornham area of Norfolk, where the wider and flatter beaches give the oyster beds better protection from the gales of winter than they would have on exposed beaches further south. But it was not always so, for in the nineteenth century native oysters *(Ostrea edulis)* were dredged and landed all around the Norfolk coast. These natives have a much flatter and rounder shell than the Pacific oysters, which are long and narrow with a thick, many-leaved shell. Since 'Pacifics' grow twice as quickly as native oysters, they are more favoured by the commercial growers. Native oysters have been around for a long time for I often find, on my local beach, fossil oysters trapped in flint nodules that date from the Cretaceous period some 85 million years ago. Evidence of live oysters being landed around the coast also comes from my own property for I live by one of the many cart gaps that wind through the sand dunes; any hole dug in the lane outside my door reveals about two foot of loose sand overlying hard packed gravel. Sandwiched between the two layers I find a carpet of flattened oyster shells where fishermen, over the years, have discarded them as they opened them up to be used, as often as not, for baiting long lines. For in earlier times oysters were the cheap food of the ordinary working man. Indeed, in 1837, Charles Dickens observed that 'poverty and oysters always seem to go together'. Using oysters for bait today would be unthinkable, for they command a good price at market and have become a luxury item in expensive London restaurants. In such places they are usually served chilled on a bed of ice and eaten raw, straight off the shell, with a squeeze of lemon juice. Wrap a tea towel around your hand to hold the oyster and open it by inserting a short, stout-bladed knife (preferably with a guard) between the two shells; cut towards the hinge and twist open, saving the juice for stock. Alternatively, as a starter, try **Angels-on-Horseback**, made by grilling the shelled oysters wrapped in streaky bacon and served on pieces of buttered toast. For the adventurous this recipe comes from '*A New System of Domestic Cookery by a Lady*', the lady being Mrs Maria Eliza Rundall (1745-1828) who tells us that in 1808 'a peck [about 436] of best native oysters may be purchased out of the boats at Billingsgate for nine shillings', which works out at about four a penny. Even if you buy them in Brancaster rather than London, they will cost you a bit more than that today.

Oyster Patties

Ingredients
Puff pastry
Oysters
Grate of nutmeg
Lemon peel
Cream
Salt and pepper
Cubes of bread

Native oysters

Method
'Put a fine puff-paste into small patty-pans, and cover with paste, with a bit of bread in each; and against they are baked have ready the following to fill with, taking out the bread. Take off the beards of the oysters, cut the other parts in small bits, put

76

them in a small tosser*, with a grate of nutmeg, the least white pepper, and salt, a morsel of lemon-peel, cut so small that you can scarcely see it, a little cream, and a little of the oyster liquor. Simmer for a few minutes before you fill.
Observe to put a bit of crust into all patties, to keep them hollow while baking.'
November 1st 1805

*The *Oxford English Dictionary* defines 'a tosser' as 'a cooking vessel, a tossing-pan', and quotes this recipe as an example of the use of the word.

Colchester oysters from the Colne estuary in Essex enjoy a long-held reputation for excellence endorsed by Henry I's royal decree in 1256. Ever since then the new season has been declared officially open with much pomp and ceremony by Colchester's mayor, usually on August 12th. This event coincides with the opening of the grouse-shooting season, referred to as 'the glorious twelfth', for much the same reasons. By mid-August both species will have completed their breeding cycle and be in their prime, thus the old adage that you should only eat shellfish when there is an 'r' in the month does make good sense. Within a couple of weeks of 'the glorious twelfth', as the nights start to draw in, other marine species start their annual breeding cycles. The fishing community has, from time immemorial, responded appropriately to this change from summer into autumn.

The Last Word on Whitefish - Don't Cook it at all!

Oysters, in this country, are traditionally eaten raw, and if you catch your own fish you have the opportunity to try something that the Japanese have been doing for centuries, eating your fish without cooking it. Please don't try it with shop bought fish unless you have a very good relationship with your fishmonger. Unlike the Japanese, our fish industry is not designed to cater safely for a raw fish diet, with the possible exception of shellfish such as oysters or catches like squid or prawns, which are frozen at source. Medical science is claiming more and more frequently that the low incidence of heart disease in Japan, despite the intense and frenetic lifestyle adopted by their city dwellers, is attributable to high levels of raw fish in their diet. If the idea doesn't appeal so be it, but if you're a fisherman who catches fresh fish my advice is to try it just once, it may be a revelation. The essence of the art, and in Japan it is an art, is to use a variety of fish and shellfish to get a contrast in colour, taste and texture, and then slice the fish into interesting shapes to provide yet more stimuli to the palate. If you're trying it for the first time, thin slicing is probably the best option to provide dainty, less daunting portions. Oily fish such as herring or mackerel are suitable just on their own for this dish, while salmon and sea trout are good for providing essential colour in the various mixes.

Ingredients

Skinless fillets of whitefish and shellfish – I suggest about 12 ounces in total of:

Option 1 - Salmon, bass, plaice and oyster
Option 2 - Grey mullet, brill, squid, and scallop
Option 3 - Sole, prawn, sea trout and oyster
Option 4 - Mackerel or herring

Sauce One

A tablespoon of Soy sauce
Zest and juice of a lime
One ounce of peeled and finely chopped ginger
5 spring onions

Sauce Two

Grated horseradish or horseradish sauce – see sauces section

Method

The choice of fish must depend on what you catch and what is available in the freezer. Prepare the sauces in advance and allow the flavours to combine for a few hours in the fridge. When you are ready, slice the fish thinly; to help you do this put the fish in the freezer for a short time.

Serving

Arrange the fish slices on small side plates with some colourful salad garnish. Put the two sauces in small bowls; to complete the picture provide chopsticks for your guests for dipping the fish. Serves 4. See Chapter 5 for other fish marinades and dressings.

Opening the oyster shell

Easing the oyster from the shell

Preparing oysters for serving

CHAPTER THREE: AUTUMN

'The man in the wilderness asked me,
how many strawberries grow in the sea?
I answered him, as I thought good,
as many as red herrings grow in the woo d.'
Traditional 1744

Introduction

With the heady days of summer fast disappearing and the holidaymakers returning to their labours, the east coast longshoreman's year starts to build to a frenzy of activity with the coming of the herring. An entire industry, now virtually defunct, was based on the annual migration of these fish to our shores, and in its time this 'home' fishing brought fame and fortune to many local families, and poverty and grief to many others.

Herring, *(Clupea harengus)* nicknamed 'silver darlings', are a most nutritious and versatile fish and the catching, processing and transportation of herring across Victorian and Edwardian Europe is a story of triumph and disaster in itself. In an age before refrigeration, pickled, smoked or 'klondyked' (boxed in ice) herring were eagerly snapped up by Roman Catholics in eastern and southern Europe who were determined to keep their faith by eating fish on a Friday, despite living many miles from the sea. Kippers and red herring proved to be an essential staple, both at home and abroad, in those lean weeks of Lent between Christmas and Easter. Every Autumn, in the last days of September, the herring drifters would start to congregate in Yarmouth and Lowestoft harbours, many of the boats coming from Scotland, having fished their way south over the summer. In their wake came a small army of Scottish fisher girls, whose arrival by train from places such as Buckie and Aberdeen announced to the world that the season's fishing was under way. Their job was to gut, salt and pack the herring in barrels for export in a traditional and carefully controlled process called the 'Scotch Cure'. Using a short knife in an action performed so quickly it resembled a conjuring trick, the fisher girls removed the guts of the fish through its gill using a short, bone-handled knife, leaving the roes intact still inside the fish. Another flick of the wrist saw the expertly graded fish unhesitatingly despatched to the appropriate barrel, where the packer would carefully arrange them to ensure that they would pack down as tightly as possible. As the fish settled in the barrels the girls topped them up with more fish from other barrels of the same size and length of cure; by packing them ever more tightly and excluding the air, the herring were preserved in their own liquor of salt and fish oil. After ten days curing, the barrels were consolidated and finally topped up with more fish, extra pickle was added and they were then sealed and branded with the quality mark of the curer. This heavy, indeed filthy work was all done on the open quayside, usually in bitter weather and the Scottish girls were tough beyond measure; they had to be to deal with the vast quantities of fish that were landed. The drifters would leave harbour in the late afternoon to steam the few miles to the fishing grounds where they cast their nets as dusk settled and then proceeded to drift with the tide throughout the night.

The best skippers could read the sea, wind and weather like a book, and used their skills to hunt out the biggest shoals using all the clues that they could muster in an age which pre-dated electronic fish-finders. One good indication was the presence of the porpoises ('blowers' the men called them) that fed on the herring; the colour and consistency of the sea water was also carefully examined, for a large shoal of herring would leave a distinctive slick of fish oil on the surface of the water. Other creatures would be migrating at this time; the Norfolk name for the tiny goldcrest is 'herring spink' (spink is a dialect word for a finch) since their arrival from Scandinavia usually coincided with the heaviest catches of herring in mid-October. Sometime during the night, perhaps towards dawn, the cry 'busky oh' would go up and the nets would be hauled and the herring shaken, or 'scudded', out of them. (Busks were the tarred canvas floats that supported the nets, hanging like a sheet in the water). If gutting and packing was hard work, then hauling and scudding nets was sheer physical drudgery, and the men would often be required to work for hours on end to recover a large catch, their arms nearly coming out of their sockets. Once aboard, the catch would be raced back to Great Yarmouth or Lowestoft to catch an early market, but the men would have only a brief respite before they began the job of unloading their catch on the quayside. The fish would be swung ashore in wicker cran baskets woven from willow wands (crans were made to a certified capacity and served to measure the quantity of fish); the fish were then tipped into swills for transporting to the auction market. Swills were also wicker baskets (*suil* is the Gaelic word for willow) and with their distinctive shape and central carrying handle they were peculiar to Great Yarmouth. By the mid 1960s the over-fishing that this intense level of activity represented was taking its toll, and the fishery collapsed. The local longshore industry continues in a much reduced form today and is relished by those in the know who appreciate the taste that fresh fish can provide, and the gourmet flavours that salt, smoke and spices give to the variously preserved forms of the species.

Drift Netting for Longshore Herring

Herring are caught by a method known as 'drift netting' where the fishermen, venturing offshore on an October evening, pay out a train of nets (known as a 'fleet') that hang like a curtain in the water, awaiting the shoals of fish. The longshoreman will time this operation carefully so that the boat, with its attendant fleet of nets, will be allowed to drift gently with the tide as it slows towards slack water, the time when the tidal current dies away as the tide turns, about two hours after the predicted high or low water. The fisherman knows that it is at this time that the herring rise up from the depths to feed on the surface plankton and he has the best opportunity to catch them. So on an autumn evening, just before dark, he will launch his boat from the beach and slowly row seawards paying out the fleet of herring nets, ensuring that they hang properly in the water. In the early part of the season, before the winter storms have stirred up the sea, fishing in the hours of darkness is essential, for the water will still be clear enough ('sheer' in Norfolk dialect) for the fish to see the net during the day. Only later in the year when the sea has been stirred to opaque soup will the longshoreman deem it to be 'thick' enough for daytime fishing. The first net to be cast will be accompanied by a solemn doffing of the cap and the words 'over for the Lord', a request for a bit of divine intervention to ensure a good catch. Having paid out the fleet, the boat and nets will slowly drift with the tide while the fishermen wait patiently for the 'swim of fish' to become entrapped.

The best time for herring catching off the east coast is at the October and November full moon. To see a net full of 'silver darlings' caught in the moonlight and slowly being drawn over the gunwale is a deeply satisfying experience described here in Norfolk as a 'shimmer o' herrin'. Even the hardest-bitten longshoreman will reflect dreamily when remembering a fine autumn evening 'fishing up the moon'.

Having drifted for half an hour or so, the net will be hauled and the fish carefully removed, but often the herring shoal in such quantities at this time of year that the nets will sink with the weight of the fish. The fisherman will then have to haul in as quickly as possible to avoid catching any more and risk capsizing the boat. When the trapped fish are found in both sides of the net, the haul is described as 'double swum'; if the net is full only of fish heads the longshoreman knows that either dogfish or seals have taken the lazy way out and helped themselves to an easy supper. Catches of twenty or thirty stone of fish are quite possible with only a small boat and two or three nets, but such gluts of fish always present the longshoreman with the problem of disposing of such bounty.

Unloading the herring on the quayside

The longshore herring tends to be smaller than its deeper water Norwegian cousin, but the timing of the autumn migration means that the fish are 'full' (i.e. they contain roes) and their oil content is still relatively high. This means that the fish are at their tastiest when eaten fresh, and in this condition they also produce the best quality kippers. Curing in smoke, salting and drying are the main means by which the autumn glut of herring has been traditionally preserved; in modern times icing and freezing are now principally employed. Converting the fish to fishmeal for use as fertiliser is now considered to be a wholly wasteful use of their valuable protein, and this practice certainly contributed to the over-fishing and subsequent collapse of the main east coast fishery in the early 1960s. The longshore fisherman has continued the tradition of herring catching and smoking, but the commercial viability of such an activity is doubtful to say the least.

The renewed interest in grilling and barbecuing oily fish, stemming from trips to Spanish and Portuguese beaches where they make the best of sardines or pilchards (they are the same species; an immature pilchard is called a sardine), may produce a resurgence of interest in the herring, but unfortunately the main herring catches here in Norfolk are made when the barbecue has long been packed away for the winter. Many a longshoreman grits his teeth to see imported sardines in the supermarkets selling for many times the pittance he can get for the almost identical, and just as tasty, locally caught herring.

Scad or Horse Mackerel

The longshoremen also find other species of fish caught in autumn herring nets and these may include mackerel, horse mackerel and shad. Horse mackerel, or scad *(Trachurus trachurus)* are similar in appearance and taste to true mackerel; they are little known in the UK but form an important fishery off the African coast. Care must be taken to avoid being pricked by their spines in removing them from the net or preparing them for the table, where they should be treated in a similar way to mackerel. The fish arrive on the Norfolk coast with the mackerel (if they arrive at all - it depends on the prevailing winds) having travelled from Africa via the Bay of Biscay and through the Channel into the North Sea, where they spend the summer feeding and getting fatter. In such a condition they are ideal for smoking and an autumn scad makes very tasty fare for the home smoker.

Mackerel   *Scad*

Shad

Shad comes in two varieties, twaite shad *(Alosa fallax)* or allis shad *(Alosa alosa);* both species are silvery in colour with a row of golden spots on their flanks, and they both look like really enormous herring. Indeed, since they are usually caught singly, the old fishermen thought they were venerable specimens of herring that led the shoals in their migration, hence catching a shad was considered a very good omen for a plentiful harvest to come. The alternative name for an allis shad is 'Queen of the Herring'. Shad are less oily than herring and taste like a cross between a herring and a white fish such as haddock. When smoked as gigantic kippers, they make a most wonderful breakfast which will satisfy the heartiest of appetites, but be warned, the twaite shad contains a plethora of bones which need careful attention when on the plate unless you proceed as follows. Remove the fillets as you would for any round fish (see p. 44), and you will find that each fillet has three lines of bones throughout its length. Run the point of a knife down each side of these lines of bones, and then use the flat of the knife blade and your thumb to grip the bones and peel them from the flesh. You may need to adjust the angle of the blade as the bones lean to one side or another, but when completed each fillet will be neatly divided into four strips held together by the skin, which you should leave on.

AUTUMN HERRING RECIPES

Shallow Fried Fresh Herring

Folks on the east coast look forward eagerly to the first herring of the year, indeed the coastal village of Hemsby regularly holds a herring festival in late summer which always attracts a good gathering on the beach to celebrate this tasty fare. Recent medical evidence has confirmed that, when eaten on a regular basis, the proteins, vitamins (A, B and D) and Omega-3 fatty acids contained in the natural oils of the fish can provide a number of health benefits. In particular Omega-3, which is not produced by the body, is an important nutrient for the human brain, and scientists tell us that a regular intake aids concentration and memory. Herring contain only low levels of cholesterol so the other major benefit of eating them includes the prevention of heart disease, so long as you don't overdo the butter in the following recipe.

Ingredients
Fresh herring, cleaned and 'snotched'
Flour
Mustard powder
Salt and Pepper
Oil or butter

Herring

Preparation
Behead and gut the herring by cutting most of the way through the head and dragging out the guts. Slit the belly and remove any roes to cook separately or retain for later use. (I freeze them in old margarine pots.) Scrape off the scales and wash the fish thoroughly under a running tap. Cut two deep gashes in the back of the herring (snotching) to prevent them from curling in the pan.

Method
Roll the fish in the seasoned flour and shallow fry in a little oil or butter for about three minutes each side. The flesh should turn from a transparent grey to an opaque white colour when done, while the skin will be browned and crispy and, some say, the tastiest part.

Serving
Serve immediately (they won't keep) with chips and bread and butter, allow 2 fish each or 3 for the very hungry.

Wind Dried Herring

Because herring are caught in the colder winter months, wind drying evolved as a method of preparing, and to some extent preserving, the fish. This method, which pre-dates the invention of refrigerators, gives the best results on one of those clear,

84

crisp late autumn days with a decided nip in the air. W. C. Hodgson in his classic treatise *The Herring and Its Fishery* describes the process, claiming, 'It is most successful in the winter months, and a frosty night in November is admirably suitable'. It is no accident that wind drying has been developed from the earliest times for the process serves to firm the flesh and bring out the very best of the flavour of these highly prized, and healthy eating fish.

Ingredients
Fresh herring
Flour
Seasoning
Butter

Method
Sprinkle the herring lightly with salt and leave them in a dish overnight. In the morning, thread the herring through the mouth and gill onto a stick and hang up the fish outdoors in a convenient place (I've seen one of my neighbours peg them out on the washing line!) to allow the wind to dry the fish. Leave for the rest of the day (watching out for seagulls) although in really cold weather time doesn't matter too much and they may still be eaten after a day or two. Prepare for cooking by opening and cleaning the fish and removing the backbone. Now that we have refrigerators a similar (though not perfect) result can be obtained by keeping the unwrapped fish in the fridge for twenty-four hours, but it's best not to try this with shop bought fish. They simply won't be fresh enough when you buy them and rapid deterioration will soon spoil the flavour, and possibly risk your health. When you are ready to cook the fish, roll them in seasoned flour and shallow fry in butter for 8-10 minutes.

Serving
Serve with hot buttered bread rolls, chips and a pot of tea.

Dutch Raw Herring

The Dutch are just as fond of herring as we are; indeed in medieval times it was they who taught us how to fish for herring on a commercial basis. Great Yarmouth's Dutch Herring Fair was an important annual event which saw dozens of Flemish fishing boats and their crews visit Yarmouth each autumn throughout the 16th, 17th and 18th centuries, a social interchange which contributed much to our Norfolk culture, especially our language. This recipe should only be attempted using really fresh herring; anything less will simply not do.

Ingredients
Fresh herring
Onion
Geneva Gin
Rye bread

Method

Gut and scale the fish, remove the head and wash thoroughly. Fillet the herring by placing the gutted fish belly-down on a board and firmly pressing along the backbone to slightly flatten and spread the fish. Turn it over and pull out and separate the backbone from the fish; it should come out whole, bringing all the side bones with it. Cut into long fillets, removing the tail. Lightly salt and refrigerate. Chop the onions into thin rings.

Serving

Chop the fillets into bite-size pieces and serve cold on a small platter surrounded with onion rings accompanied by a shot glass of Korenwein (the best Dutch Geneva gin) and bite-size pieces of rye bread. If you don't have any Geneva, try serving the fish with ice-cold vodka.

Bismarck Herring

Before the First World War, German importers visited East Anglia during the 'home fishing' to purchase many of the herring landed at Great Yarmouth and Lowestoft. The gutted fish were packed in boxes of ice, 'Klondyked', and sent off across the North Sea (then called the German Ocean) to the ports of Hamburg and Altona. The unusual name comes from the 1896 Klondyke gold rush, for the advent of the steam drifter brought the local fishing industry to a climax of success in the same way as the fortunes won in the Yukon goldfields. The iced fish were often pickled into Bismarck or rollmop herring, dishes which are still very popular all around the Baltic coast today, and have also lingered in our own local cuisine although the 'Klondyke' trade has long gone. (Nowadays the term is applied to Russian and eastern European factory ships which visit Scottish ports in Orkney and Shetland taking large quantities of fish for processing and export to their home countries). The cooking process in this case relies solely on the acidic nature of the pickle for the fish, unlike soused herring where the herring are heated and gently simmered in wine vinegar.

Ingredients

20 longshore herring
2 tablespoons of salt
2 pints of water

For the marinade

1-2 pints of white wine vinegar or cider vinegar (depending on the size of your jar)
One and a half tablespoons of pickling spice
Peppercorns
3 bay leaves
One large sliced onion
3 pickled gherkins
Onion slices
Parsley

Bay

Equipment
A wide-mouthed glass jar with an airtight lid

Method
Scale and gut the fish removing the heads and tails. Place on a board and press down on the back to flatten the fish; turn over and tease out the whole backbone. Remove any remaining pin bones (the vinegar, however, will soften any that you miss). Mix the salt and water and brine the fish for 2 hours. In the meantime make the marinade by placing all the ingredients in a pan and bringing to the boil, simmer for a couple of minutes and allow to cool. Remove the soaked herring from the brine, drain and allow to dry. Wrap each fillet around a slice of onion and piece of gherkin and arrange the rolls in a glass jar packing them in fairly tightly. Pour over the marinade, adding any leftover onion or gherkin. Put the lid on and keep in the refrigerator for 4 days, eat within another 4 days.

Serving
Drain the fish and freshen up with freshly cut onion rings and parsley garnish. For an authentic German supper, pour on a little sour cream and serve with lightly buttered rye bread, or try the mustard sauce described on p.136. Serves 6-8 people.

Supper Herring

Let me take you back to the mid-fifties when Sunday tea at Granny's just wouldn't be Sunday tea without pilchards in tomato sauce, swimming in a sea of olive oil. This recipe recreates that special taste and aroma, but by adding garlic (which Granny probably wouldn't approve of) turns these humble fish into a sumptuous hot supper dish.

Ingredients
A dozen fresh herring (or pilchards)
2 large red and green peppers
One large onion
2 cloves of garlic
6 large tomatoes
Wine or cider vinegar
2 lemons
Olive oil
Salt and pepper
Grated cheese (optional)

A distinctive Yarmouth 'swill' for carrying herring

Method
Gut and clean the herring, remove the head and take out the backbone by flattening the fish on a board and teasing it from the flesh. De-seed and chop the peppers and tomatoes into small dice. Finely slice the onion, garlic cloves and lemons. Sweat the vegetables in the olive oil in a large flat pan; adjust the seasoning to taste. Add the

wine vinegar and lemons and simmer for a couple of minutes before adding the herring. Put a lid on the pan (or cover with foil) and simmer for another 15-20 minutes, either on the top or in a hot oven. Finish off by browning under the grill; gratinate if preferred.

Serving
Serve with waxy, boiled potatoes and hot, toasted garlic bread. Serves 6.

SMOKING TECHNIQUES

Smoking is an important process by which our forebears sought to preserve shoaling fish, especially the herring. As we all know, herring are highly perishable, and even in the cooler autumn temperatures they will not remain palatable for more than a few days without some form of preservative treatment such as drying, salting or smoking. It was discovered in very early times that hanging the fish in a stream of smoke drove off much of the moisture contained in the flesh, thus inhibiting the growth of moulds and fungi, while the active ingredients of the smoke itself (pyrolignins) had a preservative effect on the fish. Just when, or how this important discovery was made we can't be sure, but it must surely have followed shortly after the discovery of the process of cooking with fire. Techniques soon evolved for refining this process with the addition of brining, where the water content of the cells of the fish is reduced and transferred to the brine by a process of osmosis resulting from the high concentration of salt in the mixture. Tall kilns (called 'kills' in Norfolk) for producing smoked fish became a common feature of all east coast towns in the medieval period, one of the first examples in this country of industrialised food-processing. In Great Yarmouth one such kill was actually built into the medieval town wall; today it is an interesting museum and commercial pottery. Just up the road, a large Victorian Curing Works has also been converted to the highly-acclaimed Time and Tide Museum, largely dedicated to the herring. The brining and smoking process was intended primarily to preserve the fish, but it also had the effect of drastically, and pleasantly, altering the taste of the flesh. This is why smoked products are still enjoyed today, despite the fact that we now have far more effective means, such as canning or refrigeration, to stop fish rapidly spoiling.

Make Your Own Smokehouse

The home smoker does not need to go to the expense of building a permanent brick-built smokehouse to produce tasty and nutritious products.

Just about any large container can easily be converted into a smoker and fitted out with racks to hold the fish; upturned whisky barrels have traditionally been used in Scotland to produce both Arbroath Smokies and Finnan Haddies. A perfectly usable and easily dismantled smoker can be made using a couple of hundred ordinary household bricks. Initially loose-lay them into a waist-high circular tower, about three feet (one metre) in diameter, leaving small gaps between the bricks to allow a circulation of air. Build in a metal plate near the base on which to place the sawdust, leaving enough room underneath to take a gas burner or charcoal fire; in both cases leave out a few bricks in a couple of layers to allow access. Have more bricks to hand so that, as you hang the fish in the tower, you can add further layers of bricks, building up to around chest height. Build in a grill halfway up the structure to catch any fish that may drop off the wooden rods (speets or baulks) on which you hang the fish. Place these rods across the bricks at the mouth of the tower; use off-cuts of timber to fill the gaps and provide a level surface on which to build up more layers of bricks as required. Make the baulks from one-inch (25mm) square battens of soft timber long enough to span the brick tower. Bang into the timber two-inch (5cm) long 'lost head' nails, spaced at two-inch centres ensuring that they protrude right through the wood. These can then be turned up at the ends to produce hooks on which to spike the fish that have been cut for kippers. Speets are smooth, slender, wooden rods which are threaded through the mouth and gill of the herring when curing them into bloaters. The bottom layer of fish should be no closer than eighteen inches (45cm) to the smouldering saw-dust, while the number of further layers will be dictated by the quantity of fish you have to smoke and the stability of the tower; four layers is about the limit. Put a cover over the top to retain the smoke in the tower for as long as possible.

Choose a location for your smoker far enough from the house to keep the smoke at bay, but near enough for you to keep an eye on things. The best times for smoking are those slightly damp and misty autumn days with just a light breeze that will help to keep the smoke flowing. You will find that you will need to tend the fire and replenish the sawdust at regular intervals; I usually spend the time in between tidying up the garden and doing all the things that never got done in the summer.

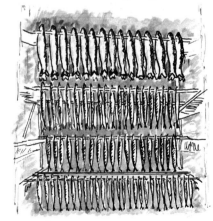

Herring speeted up for curing into bloaters

Home Smoked Kippers and Bloaters

It was during the First World War that kippers were first dyed to give them their distinctive browny hue, a measure of economy that meant that smoking times could be shortened and subsequent weight-loss reduced. But, as with every short cut, a price had to be paid, in this case the loss of both flavour and texture. As a result, kippers started to be regarded as factory-produced second class food and something not to be taken seriously in the culinary world. Towards the end of the twentieth century a resurgence of interest in natural foodstuffs, which were not produced on an assembly line, has seen every supermarket put undyed oak-smoked kippers on their fishmongers' slabs and undoubtedly they are much better than the plastic-coated kipper fillets of the 1960s. But nothing can compare with the ones that you produce yourself from fish straight from the sea, and the following recipe explains just how to produce these smoky delights.

Ingredients
About 100 very fresh longshore herring
One and a half kilos of salt
A sack of oak sawdust

Equipment
A large plastic garden tub with handles
Measuring jug
Wooden stirrer
Some form of smoker fitted with racks to hold the fish

Preparing the Fish
The herring must be obtained very fresh, preferably from the boat; although the gutted and scaled fish can be kept in a freezer prior to processing as long as they go into the freezer virtually still wriggling! Divide the catch as follows:

Largest fish for kippers - usually about 25% of the catch
Smallest fish for eating immediately - usually about 15%
Medium fish for bloaters - usually about 60%

Kippering a fish that is too small will produce an over-dried inedible result; if you can't eat all the smallest fish, freeze them for later or give them away. Kippers are prepared by cutting along the backbone from head to tail. Open out like a book and remove the guts and any roes. Remove the gills and scales and run a knife along the backbone to remove the blood vessel lying next to it. Leave the head and tail on. Wash thoroughly. Prepare the bloaters (the name comes from the Scandinavian *blotfisk* and means 'soft' or 'soaked' fish) by slitting the belly, and removing the guts and roes. Leave the head and tail on and wash well. Technically a bloater should be cured with the guts intact for eating immediately, but with freezer storage this method gives a better result. Reserve the roes; I usually save them in old margarine pots for freezing (filling them half full is about right for most uses) making sure that the pots contain an even mixture of hard and soft. However, I will usually do one or two pots of just soft roes for dishes that specifically call for them.

Salting
Prepare a saturated salt mixture by dissolving the whole one and a half kilo (3.3 pounds) packet in 12 pints of ice cold water; this will be sufficient for a hundred fish. Brine the fish for one hour (50 minutes only for small fish). The salt concentration and the timing are critical to achieving the best result. Remove the fish and discard the brine.

Cold Smoking
Air dry the fish and rack up in the smoker, kippers closest to the smoke. Use only oak sawdust; slightly damp chain-saw chippings work well, but avoid any that are badly oiled. Light a small fire with sticks and paper then smother it with sawdust and allow it to smoulder slowly. If the sawdust keeps going out, keep the smoke flowing with a small charcoal fire or gas burner placed under the metal sheet on which you put the sawdust. Avoid too much heat as this will cook the fish and they will fall off the baulks. The fish should remain cold throughout, with the temperature in the smokehouse constantly maintained at less than 70°F. Aim to trickle smoke for at least six hours; longer won't do any harm.

Yield
Expect to produce about twenty-five kippers, thirty golden cure bloaters, and thirty silver cure bloaters. The fish will appear a much lighter colour than the dyed, commercially produced product; the typical kipper colour will fully develop when they are cooked. Gently wipe off any smuts from the fish and pack in pairs for the freezer. Placing then skin to skin will make them easier to separate, as will interleaving them with plastic film. Eat immediately for the best flavour, especially the lightly cured bloaters. Kippers and bloaters will keep well for about three months in the freezer.

The Secret of How to Eat a Kipper

It is an undeniable fact that herring are full of thin wiry bones that not only get in the way of the delicious flesh but are not good to eat, as anyone will tell you who gets one stuck in the throat! Avoidance is essential, and the best way to achieve this is to understand how the fish is put together. Then you can easily dissemble it on the plate. In preparing the kipper the fish is cut down its backbone exposing the interior flesh, but this also has the effect of ensuring that the tasty meat lies under a maze of bones. The result is that as soon as you try to remove the parts you *do* want to eat, they get hopelessly tangled up in the parts that you *don't*. The secret of eating a kipper is to place it skin side up on the plate, sliding the blade of the knife under the skin will then easily remove it. The part you want to eat is then neatly exposed and lies on top of the bones so that you can lift the fillets off the bones, leaving the offending articles on the plate. If you do get a bone stuck in your throat, try alternating sips of lemon juice (which will soften the bone) and lumps of dry bread which should dislodge it, but don't be ashamed to seek medical help sooner rather than later if this fails.

COLD-SMOKED FISH RECIPES

Kippers Hors D'Oeuvres and Melba Toast

Home-cured, oak-smoked kippers, like smoked salmon, need no further cooking. Slice the kipper fillets thinly with a sharp knife, sprinkle with lemon juice and serve with bread and butter or Melba toast for an incomparable gourmet treat. Named in honour of the opera singer Dame Nellie Melba, the snack is said to have been invented by the famous chef Auguste Escoffier to tempt the famous diva's palate during her illness in 1897. The toast is simply made according to *Schott's Food & Drink Miscellany* as follows:

'Lightly toast slices of bread and, while they are still warm, slice them through their middles into two thin halves. Re-toast the halves (a warm oven is ideal) until the edges start to curl.'

Grilled Kippers and Bloaters

Both kippers and bloaters can be grilled with a dab of butter under a high heat for three to five minutes; remove the heads if preferred. Serve with toast or bread and butter. Alternatively, slowly shallow fry in butter, especially if the fish have been caught and cured later in the season (after Christmas) when the oil content of the herring will be much less than an autumn caught specimen. With both grilling and frying, gourmets say the best method for kippers is to cook them in pairs, putting flesh to flesh with a small pat of butter between them. As the sandwich of kippers is turned the oil of one runs into the other producing a sort of basting action and superlative flavour. A third method, which may help to reduce the cooking smell, is to stand the kippers upright in a jug of boiling water for a few minutes and either eat straight away or place under the grill for a little more cooking. This will soften the flesh of a hard smoked fish and can be effective for any kippers that have been hung low down in the smokehouse near to the fire, becoming extra dry in the smoking process.

Red Herring

The jug method is essential in preparing heavily-salted red herring which are usually given three or four smokings over a two-three week period leaving them highly

92

coloured, highly aromatic and as stiff as boards. This medieval technique pre-dates kippering and bloatering by several centuries. Tales abound on the east coast of the remarkable keeping qualities of red herring; one favourite describes a situation where a few 'reds' are inadvertently left in a corner of the smokehouse after the curer receives his call to arms and goes off to war (the Crimean, Boer or Great War - take your pick). On his return some years later, he finds to his delight that his 'reds' taste just as good as if they had been smoked the previous week. A good 'red', say the aficionados, should always need more than one soaking to remove all the salt, but the result is a gourmet treat, definitely not for the faint-hearted! Traditionally publicans served 'reds' to their customers for toasting on a fork over an open fire, in the knowledge that the salty fare would invoke a powerful thirst that only the consumption of many pints of beer would properly quench. A cosy pub bearing the name 'The Red Herring' is still to be found in Great Yarmouth, but don't expect to find 'reds' on their menu.

Salmagundi

Salmagundi (or salmagundy) comes from the French *salmigondis* meaning a medley or miscellany, and this ancient, but interesting assemblage of minced morsels is obviously deliberately designed to stimulate the palate, perhaps as a relief from the generally monotonous diet that winter enforced. The eighteenth century date of the recipe well demonstrates the antiquity of red herring and the dish is perhaps a forerunner of what we now call Steak Tartare.

Ingredients
Veal or chicken
Red Herring
Minced raw beef
Apple
Onion
Anchovies
Lemon
Olive oil
Mustard
Vinegar
Salt and pepper   *Commercial smoking*

'Take a little cold veal, or cold fowl, the white part, free of fat and skin, mince it very fine; take either a red herring, a pickled herring, or three or four anchovies, whichever you please; if herring skin and bone it; peel and shred small a couple of onions, core, pare, and shred two apples, a little hung beef minced fine. Lay it on a dish in small heaps, each ingredient separate; put a few anchovies into the middle of the dish. Garnish with lemon. Eat with oil, mustard and vinegar.'

Elizabeth Taylor '*The Art of Cookery*' 1769

Why Do Herring Migrate?

Longshore herring are members of one specific 'tribe' of North Sea herring, identifiable as being smaller than other tribes, which include Norwegian and Baltic herring. The longshores come to the Norfolk coast spawning grounds to lay their eggs where they often form thick carpets on the seabed. However, the creation of the east coast herring fishery, the 'Home Fishing', relied on the annual migration of another tribe of herring which shoaled in vast quantities, indeed the meaning of the word herring comes from Old High German *hegri,* a host or army. The shoals move south through the North Sea over the summer and gather in the autumn months to feed on the banks lying off the Norfolk coast, where they form easy prey for the fishing drifters so that many never make it to their spawning grounds in the Sandettie region of the English Channel. But why is it that these herring migrate year after year? Certainly the funnel shape of the North Sea serves to concentrate the fish, and this funnel shape is dictated by the underlying geology of the basal rocks, which may also dictate the migration pattern in another way. Remember that the North Sea only formed at the end of the last Ice Age, around ten thousand years ago. Prior to its inundation, the area we now call the North Sea was a vast plain teeming with wildlife such as deer, elephant and rhinoceros. Through this wooded paradise ran an enormous river estuary with many tributaries draining the European mainland through what we now call the Straits of Dover. Human activity at the time is indicated by a Neolithic harpoon which was retrieved by a trawler in the 1930s from peat beds forming the Dogger Bank (in the middle of the North Sea) showing that the area must once have been land. From this, and other evidence, we now know that what was once land and river is now sea, but the herring may not know this. Many species of fish live in both marine and freshwater conditions at different times in their life cycles, returning to the place of their birth to spawn. The salmon is perhaps the best known of these anadromous species as they unerringly travel to the headwaters of rivers; leaping up the river rapids in a most spectacular and determined fashion. It is thought that the herring's genes also dictate that they must migrate back to the place of their birth in order to spawn and reproduce themselves, so they too relentlessly follow the course of this long lost river, even though that freshwater estuary has long ceased to exist and the herring now live an entirely marine life. In support of this theory a larger relative of the herring, the shad, still swims up estuaries to spawn where they may be caught far from the sea. There are two sorts of shad, Allis Shad *(Alosa alosa)* and Twaite Shad *(Alosa fallax)* both of which are caught off our coast but not in commercial quantities. Larger than a herring, they are dubbed 'California Herring' by the Hemsby fishermen, presumably on the grounds that anything American is larger than life and that the village of that name is located nearby. California was named following the lucrative discovery of a pot of gold coins in the cliffs, towards the middle of the 19th century, at the time of the California gold rush.

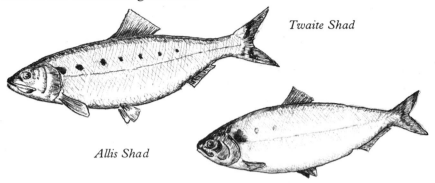

Twaite Shad

Allis Shad

Exploiting the Herring Migration: The Home Fishing

By the time of the great Klondyke gold rush, at the turn of the 19th century, Norfolk's herring fishery was going through a bonanza comparable to that in the Alaskan goldfields, with seasonal landings comprising millions and millions of fish. The fishery peaked in 1913 when some 1,000 drifters from both England and Scotland landed 824,213 cran of herring at Great Yarmouth's fish quay. Crans are carefully made wicker baskets which when certified to the correct capacity were used as a measure for herring. In 1852 the Board of Fisheries fixed the size of crans at 37½ gallons, equivalent to 28 stone or approximately 1,100 fish; which means that an incredible 906 million herring were caught and landed in the last months of 1913.

However, such successes were not sustainable and there were lean years such as 1916 when only 12,289 cran were landed. The intervention of the Second World War forced the herring drifters to limit fishing operations (many were armed and used for mine-laying); smaller catches eased the situation for a few years and allowed the shoals to recover partially. Better landings were thus made in the immediate post-war period, but they soon dwindled and by the early 1960s poor figures were repeated year on year and in 1963 no English boats landed herring at Yarmouth. The demise of the fishery finally came in 1967 when the last of the Scottish boats abandoned the town and the market for herring crashed, leaving only the longshoremen to carry on.

Since herring are shoaling fish there is usually no half measure in catching them; either the herring tumble into the longshoreman's nets in quantity, or they are not there at all. Every herring fisherman knows that if the first 'look-on' reveals only a few fish he must either move to different waters or pack up and go home. However there is good evidence that some seasons are better than others, and W.C Hodgson in *The Herring and Its Fishery* notes what at first may be a surprising coincidence, that vintage wine seasons occur in the same years as a plentiful herring harvest. The cause, he says, is the extra sunlight and warmth produced over a good summer, which falls on the land, swelling the grapes to bursting with extra sweetness. This same sunlight also falls on the sea, promoting the growth of the minute sea creatures upon which the herring feed. The equation is simple; more food sustains more herring, the fish are thus fitter and better able to survive the rigours of life in the sea, and the sea itself is a more benign environment in good summers, thus ensuring high survival rates. It all adds up to bumper catches in the autumn and, since the herring are but part of the food chain of the sea, this bounty is reflected in catches of other fish as well.

The Language of Herring

Herring may be caught all around the North Sea, Irish Sea and Baltic coasts so, not surprisingly, countries which border these seas have their own word for herring, but less surprisingly, given the constant interchange which naturally occurs between fishing communities, they all use basically the same word to describe the fish. So the French call them *hareng,* the Dutch use *haring*, in Germany they are *hering;* the Italians, who import many cured herring, call them *aringa* and the Spanish and Portuguese *arenque*. The Scandinavians however use variants of the word *sild* for the fish, while in Polish they are *sledz*. Undoubtedly many of these languages would have been heard in the Yarmouth Herring Fair, which saw fisher folk from all around the North Sea congregating in the port every autumn. This explains why, in Norfolk dialect, we always refer to the fish in both singular and plural as herring, not herrings. This follows the Flemish language, which doesn't require the addition of an 's' or 'es' to pluralise a word, a convention also occasionally adopted in English, as when we refer to sheep or deer.

In former times, herring were graded into eight different categories according to their roe content and length, using distinctive terms as follows:

Large Full Herring – fish full of milt or roe, not less than 11 inches long
Full Herring - fish with milt or roe in them not less than 10 inches long
Large Spent Herring – fish that have spawned, not less than 10 inches long
Filling Herring – maturing fish, not less than 10 inches long
Medium Herring – maturing fish not less than 9½ inches long

Matfull Herring – fish with milt and roe not less than 9 inches long
Matties – young maturing fish not less than 9 inches long
Spents – herring that have shed their milt or roe
    Matfull and Matties come from the Dutch word for maiden, *maatjes,* meaning a young, fat virgin herring.

Nearly the Last Words on Herring

As well as our cuisine and our language, the herring has entered into other aspects of our culture. The unique structure of a herring's backbone has been copied by countless weavers, and also, especially in the eastern counties, by bricklayers, in the traditional 'herring-bone pattern'. The herring gull *(Larus argentatus)* undoubtedly got its name from its preferred form of lunch. As we have seen above, herring were graded by their length, and this unique form of measurement gave rise to the traditional Norfolk saying that 'Cromer church is a herring and a half higher than Winterton church'. Both of these lofty coastal edifices owe their existence to the wealth of the local herring industry. 'Every herring should hang by its own head', is another way of saying that all should stand on their own merits. The *Oxford English Dictionary* tells us that a derogatory term for a Scandinavian is a 'herring-snapper', whilst 'herring pond' is an equally derogatory term for the mighty Atlantic Ocean. Herring are well celebrated in song as Percy Montrose's classic gold rush tale reveals that for his miner's darling daughter, 'herring boxes without topses, sandals were for Clementine'. Ewan MacColl's emotive folk song 'The Shoals of Herring' quickly established itself as the definitive refrain of the Home Fishing, even though it was only composed in the dying days of the industry for a ground-breaking BBC radio programme in the late 1950s. The term 'dead as a herring' means most certainly dead and derives from the fact that herring expire as soon as they are pulled from the sea. The distinctive shape of the kipper, and perhaps its hue, gave us that multi-coloured 1960s fashion statement the 'kipper tie', whilst fans of the outer space sitcom 'Red Dwarf' will know that one of its heroes constantly urges all and sundry to 'smoke me a kipper, I'll be back for breakfast'. On the literary front, any resident of Great Yarmouth is, of course, a 'Yarmouth bloater' and Clara Peggotty, in Charles Dickens' *David Copperfield* was proud to call herself one. 'White herring' is what Norfolk people call fresh herring, as distinct from 'red herring', which were perhaps first celebrated in literature by Thomas Nashe's 1599 play *'In Praise of Red Herring'*. The distinctive aroma of red herring and its ability to distract hounds from the scent prompted the phrase 'to draw a red herring across his path', meaning to distract someone from their true purpose. Finally, we find that while the phrase 'neither fish, flesh, fowl nor good red herring', means 'neither one thing nor another', it does firmly place these highly-smoked delicacies in a distinctive, and well-deserved class of their own.

OTHER SMOKED FISH RECIPES

Cold-Smoked Sea Trout

Here is a gourmet dish that very few have the privilege of trying and with a texture and flavour that will relegate the taste of shop-bought, farmed, smoked salmon to the realms of fatty brown carpet underlay!

Method
Gut and fillet the sea trout (a 2-3 pound fish is ideal) and salt the sides as described for herring. Give them a good hour and a half in the brine, a little longer for larger fillets. Being quite heavy, the fillets are prone to falling off the normal baulks used for kippers, so poke a sharp cocktail stick through the thicker end of the fillet making sure you pierce a good firm bit of skin. Then thread string around the ends of the sticks and hang the fish in the smoker. Allow the fillets to dry until a sticky 'pellicule' forms on the flesh, then cold-smoke for 6-8 hours depending on size. Remove from the smoker and when really cool slice thinly with a sharp knife, removing any remaining pin bones. Smoked sea trout freezes well and I have successfully kept whole fillets in the freezer for a year or more with no loss of flavour or texture.

Serving
Serve with a twist of lemon and brown bread and butter, or assemble with cream cheese and sliced gherkins as part of an hors d'oeuvre platter. Use leftover fish scraps and cream cheese to make a pâté in the same way as smoked herring or mackerel (see below).

Smoked Sea Trout and Leek Tray Bread

Tray bread is a close relative of Italian pizza, but by using a shallow tray lined with dough you can include liquid ingredients, such as this wonderful soured cream savoury custard, which simply wouldn't adhere properly to the normal flat bread base of a pizza. The traditional Italian dish uses *pancetti*, thinly-sliced smoked bacon as the main ingredient, but this smoked fish alternative is even better, especially with the addition of a few anchovies. But be warned, as with any hot bread dish, the ensemble is rich and very moreish!

Ingredients

The Bread
2 cups (8 ounces) of unbleached strong bread flour

One egg
One ounce of butter
One teaspoon of salt
One teaspoon of dried yeast
6 tablespoons of water

The Filling
4-5 leeks washed and thinly sliced
2 tablespoons of olive oil
4 ounces of thinly sliced cold-smoked sea trout (smoked salmon, mackerel or kipper are good alternatives)
A small can of anchovy fillets
5 fluid ounces of soured cream
5 tablespoons of milk
2 eggs, lightly beaten
One tablespoon of freshly chopped basil leaves
Salt and pepper

Method
Use a bread machine to make the dough, lightly oil a shallow square baking tin. Pre-heat the oven to 190°C/365°F. Gently fry the leeks in the oil for about five minutes until nicely softened, set aside to cool. Mix the soured cream, milk and beaten eggs in a pouring jug, add the basil and seasoning, but go easy with the salt for both the sea trout and anchovies are likely to be quite salty. Soured cream is readily available from supermarkets, or you can make your own by adding a few drops of lemon juice and tartaric acid to single cream. When the dough is ready place it on a floured board, knock it back gently and then roll it out to a rectangle slightly larger than your tin. Line the tin with the dough pinching it up the sides, try to keep an even thickness all round. Scatter the leeks, sea trout and anchovies over the dough, pour on the custard mixture and bake for around thirty minutes until the dough is nicely golden and the leeks are just showing brown and crisped edges.

Serving
Serve warm with a simple salad of dressed leaves, or if you are really hungry use as an accompaniment to a bowl of homemade fish soup (see Chapter 5) with a small pot of soured cream on the side.
Serves 4.

Sea Trout

Smoked Mackerel

Ingredients
Fresh mackerel *(Scomber scombrus)*
Salt
Peppercorns (crushed)

The fish should be filleted from the bone, washed, brined and cold-smoked in much the same way as herring - delicious served hot or cold with bread and butter and lemon garnish. Roll the flesh side in crushed pepperc orns if preferred.

Smoked Flatfish

Smoked flatfish are rarely seen in this country, but go to Esbjerg in Denmark and you will find their local delicacy, smoked dab *(bakskule)*, offered on all the fishmongers' slabs. Similarly, smoked flounders are relished all along the Baltic coast, indeed some would claim that smoking them is about the only way to make them palatable! Remove the head with a V-shaped cut and draw out the guts. Rinse thoroughly and brine for about 40 minutes. Hang in the smokehouse in the usual way and cold-smoke for up to 6 hours. Remove the skin prior to serving.

Smoked Mackerel or Kipper Pâté with Norfolk Hollow Biscuits

Storing home-smoked kippers or mackerel in the freezer can sometimes cause you to de-frost more fish than is required; this is a useful recipe to use up any leftovers and is also a further preservation process. Fish that have been damaged during the smoking process are ideal for this recipe, or those that have been badly cut, leaving them with a forked tail (something which in former times wouldn't be sold for fear of associating too closely with that other owner of a forked tail, 'Old Nick').

Ingredients
4 kippers, mackerel fillets, cured herring, smoked sea trout or smoked salmon
2 ounces of butter
4 ounces of Philadelphia cheese
2 teaspoons of creamed horseradish sauce (see p. 135)
Black pepper
Pinch of paprika
Juice of half a lemon

Method
Grill or bake the fish in the usual way for 5-10 minutes. Allow to cool and remove the head, skin, and as many of the bones as possible from the flaked flesh of the fish. Add half the butter and all the cheese. Mix thoroughly with a fork or blend if preferred (this will break up any remaining fine bones). Fold in the horseradish and season with the black pepper and lemon juice (which will also serve to soften any

remaining bones). Spoon into two or three ramekin dishes, picking out any missed bones as you do so. Clarify the remaining butter by heating gently and removing the foam that forms on the top. Seal the pots with a layer of butter; add a shake of paprika for colour. Cool and eat within 2-3 days or label and freeze. You can dispense with butter to seal the pot by capping it with an airtight plastic lid; I use the tops off empty tubes of Pringles crisps.

Serving

Spread thickly on hot, buttered toast, the pâté makes a special tea-time treat; add spice and colour with a bunch of watercress For an interesting starter or delicious canapé with a truly Norfolk pedigree, spread on halves of Hollow Biscuits (Norfolk Nobs), a form of crisp bread brought to Norfolk by the Danish invaders of the eighth century. The crunch of these twice-baked traditional rusks (see p. 36) makes a delicious contrast to the smoothness of the cream-based pâté. For larger dinner parties try offering a unique 'smokehouse starter' comprising three different sorts of pâté stuffed into rolls of thinly sliced kipper, mackerel and smoked sea trout fillets secured with cocktail sticks.

Hot-smoking

To build a hot-smoker you will need to fashion an oven with an external source of heat. I use an old Dutch oven which I bought for a song in a country sale years ago; I recently saw a similar one in an antique shop with an asking price of £78! You may also try using a large saucepan or Dixie with a tight-fitting lid; whatever you use will get very smoky and will invariably need to be used out of doors.

Prepare your smoker by selecting a metal bowl of suitable diameter and placing it into the saucepan. This bowl (a foil pie dish is ideal and can be thrown away afterwards) will contain about a quarter of a pint of water together with any herbs or oils you may use to impart special flavours to your dish. Remove the handle of an old wire chip basket and place this upside down over the water bowl, whilst in the very bottom of the smoker around the water dish you will pile a generous half-inch (25mm) thick layer of sawdust to produce the smoke. Carefully place your food on the wire mesh of the chip basket, put on the lid and apply heat to your smoker using a barbecue or gas burner. Don't be timid with the heat; you should aim to get the temperature inside the smoker above 80°C to ensure that your food is thoroughly cooked. The sawdust will soon smoulder producing smoke, which will mingle with the steam produced from the water, and thus thoroughly permeate the food, keeping it succulent and moist.

With a little practice you will get used to adjusting the cooking time to the heat of your burner. As a guide, an inch (25mm) thick fish steak will be well cooked within 8-10 minutes while a small whole chicken will take about

40 minutes. Remember that the smoke will blacken the food, giving it a burnt appearance; don't let this fool you into thinking that the food is overdone. Apply the usual fork test; if the juices run clear, this indicates that the inside of the food has been thoroughly cooked.

If you find collecting all the bits and pieces described above a bit too much, a trip to a good garden centre will usually secure a commercially produced smoker These are imported from the USA, and are usually large enough to take a good-sized turkey, Americans' favourite smokehouse fare.

Sawdust, Herbs and Oils

You should avoid pine sawdust as this will produce an unpleasant taste, but almost any other hardwood will do fine. Some expatriate American acquaintances of mine will use nothing but hickory and have resorted to buying and chipping hammer handles from the DIY store to obtain a supply! Fruitwoods such as apple or pear will impart a pleasant flavour, while in France the acrid smoke of vine trimmings is a favourite for specialities such as John Dory *(Zeus faber)*, a distinctive flatfish that, like the haddock, shows the thumbprint of St Paul on its flanks. Rosemary, sage, lavender, mint or tiny quantities of the oils of these herbs can be used to great effect to flavour the food. The Chinese hot-smoke fish and shellfish over a mixture of green tea and herbs; try using Earl Grey tea, which is scented with bergamot.

HOT-SMOKED FISH RECIPES

Smoke-Roasted Sea Trout in a Butter Sauce

Just about any fish can be hot-smoked (see smoked cod and cream) but the wild salmon or sea trout is the species preferred by all the best fish restaurants. I well remember the first time I tasted this dish in the Blue Schooner Restaurant at Kinsale Head, a small fishing village a few miles outside Cork in the Republic of Ireland. The plethora of restaurants that crowd the small harbour there, have a reputation second to none for the quality of their maritime fare, with a tariff to test the deepest of pockets; fortunately for me my visit was funded by an EU research project! For this recipe you can elect to prepare the whole thing from raw ingredients or prepare the stock in advance and use fillets that you have previously hot-smoked. If you don't have your own supply of sea trout, you may purchase good quality hot-smoked salmon fillets from specialist smokers; look on the internet for supplies by post.

Ingredients
4 thick fillets of hot-smoked sea trout
4 rashers of streaky bacon

Court bouillon stock
One large onion
One leek
2 sticks of celery
One bulb of fennel
4 carrots
Half a head of garlic
8 peppercorns
One teaspoon of coriander
One star anise
One bay leaf
Tablespoon of mixed herbs
Cup of white wine

For the sauce
One pint of stock (see above)
6 ounces of unsalted butter
Lemon juice
Salt and pepper

Garnish
Watercress
Salad leaves
Boiled potatoes

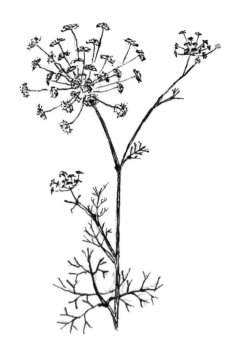

Fennel

Method

Gut and fillet the sea trout and divide into portions. Hot-smoke the inch-thick portions for around 10 minutes as described above, and either use straight away or allow to cool in the fridge until you are ready to assemble the final dish. Alternatively freeze in plastic bags interleaved with layers of plastic film to prevent sticking, but use within a couple of months for the best flavour.

Prepare the stock in advance by chopping all the vegetables into small cubes; place in a saucepan and cover with water, adding the garlic, peppercorns, coriander and star anise. Bring to the boil and simmer for 10 minutes, then add the fresh herbs and give it 3 or 4 minutes more, finally adding the white wine. Immediately remove from the heat; allow to cool and marinate for a couple of days in the fridge. Strain prior to use, any excess can be frozen and stored as ice cubes.

Make the sauce by reducing the stock with a hard boil until it turns thick and dark. Remove from the heat and add the butter, return to a very low heat and whisk the mixture until it foams to a light frothy texture. Add the lemon juice, adjust the seasoning and keep warm.

Fry or grill the bacon until really crispy and allow to cool while you warm the previously smoked fillets in a hot frying pan or fierce grill, 3 minutes should be plenty.

103

Serving

Crumble the crispy bacon onto the hot fillets floating in a sea of the sauce. Serve with simple boiled potatoes and salad with watercress garnish.

Hot-Smoked Codling and Cream

This recipe is based on 'Arbroath smokies', a speciality of the Aberdeen coast where small haddock (occasionally whiting) are beheaded, split and tied by the tails in pairs for brining and hot-smoking over oak shavings. Haddock is not caught in large quantities off the Norfolk coast, but I use this technique for any small codling that I catch in the herring nets. The fish are smoked at a higher temperature (up to 85°C) than the 'cold-smoking' technique employed for herring; they become partially cooked in the process with dark coppery brown skins, while the flesh turns to a flaky, creamy opaqueness. Tying the tails together and hanging them over the baulks rather than 'pricking them on' is essential to avoid them falling from the hooks as the flesh cooks. Smoke them for about 2 hours. Bass and mullet can also be smoked in this way; larger specimens can be split and filleted having been given a little longer in the brine bath. If you don't have your own supply of smoked fish, shop-bought smoked cod or haddock works nearly as well, for cream and any smoked whitefish invariably proves a successful marriage.

Ingredients
4 or 5 smoked codling
4 or 5 tomatoes
Double cream
Salt and pepper
Parmesan cheese

Method
Skin, de-seed and finely chop the tomatoes, place in a single portion soufflé dish. Season well and add a generous layer of flaked smoked fish. Top up with the double cream, add a sprinkle of cheese and bake in a hot oven until lightly browned.
    Serves 6.

Buckling

Buckling (the name comes from the German *buckling*, plural *bucklinge)* are whole hot-smoked herring with the head and guts are removed but the roes left in. To prepare buckling, first scale the fish and make a small cut across the vent to cut through the lower end of the gut. Then, holding the fish on the board as if it were swimming through the water, proceed to cut off the head; as you complete the cut, slide the knife sideways and drag out the guts, leaving any roes in the fish. Brine the fish in the same way as kippers or bloaters and allow to drain. Place on a wire mesh rack in the smoker (don't try to hang them on baulks as they will soon fall off as the flesh cooks) and hot-smoke them for about 40 minutes to an hour. The temperature in the hot-smoker should be in excess of 85°C to ensure that the fish are cooked through and showing a wonderful crinkled golden colour. Remove them from the racks and eat immediately. Try serving them for high tea with toast and scrambled eggs, or allow to cool and eat with brown bread and butter. They eat well hot or cool; they won't keep, however, so freeze any excess as soon as they are cold and eat within 3 months.

The Uncommon Life Cycle of the Common Eel

Perhaps the most remarkable example of genetic drive in fish is the curious life cycle of the common eel *(Anguilla anguilla)*. The eel lives for much of its life in inland freshwater lakes such as Broadland, and only returns to the sea to breed, hundreds of miles away across the Atlantic in the Sargasso Sea between Bermuda and the Leeward Islands. Having spawned, the exhausted adults die, but their eggs and larvae stream back towards Europe carried by surface currents, principally the North Atlantic Drift. The larvae look nothing like eels but resemble willow leaves. During their three-year journey they grow larger, then at about three inches (8cm) in length they metamorphose into transparent glass eels as they approach the coast. Finally, they become pigmented and in the spring these elvers move in their thousands into the estuaries of the UK and the European mainland, where they are snapped up by hungry gourmets. Why do they undertake such a tremendous journey? Part of the answer lies in the geology of the underlying rocks. During the late Carboniferous period (some 250 million years ago) the continents of Africa and America were joined, but due to continental drift they slowly started to move away from each other, forming the Atlantic Ocean. As a result of volcanic activity at the mid-Atlantic ridge, the lava spewing onto the seabed forced the two sides of the ridge apart, creating new ocean floor in a process known as 'seafloor spreading'; something which continues to this day at a rate of about one centimetre per year. Genetically locked into their migration, the poor old eels had to travel further and further to reach their spawning grounds, their only adaptation being in the rate of growth of the larvae to adulthood as the distances, and time-spans, grew larger and larger. (American eels also spawn in the Sargasso Sea but they turn left to the US and reach their rivers, and maturity, in a fraction of the time).Thus, at the time of the September and October full moons, the eels living in the dykes and marshes of east Norfolk's Horsey levels, just a stone's throw from the sea, are prompted to start their migration towards the western Atlantic. But many never make it, for where Heigham Sound and Kendal Dyke flow into the Thurne, just above Potter Heigham, there is an ancient eel sett. There were once many such eel traps in Norfolk but this is the last one remaining, comprising a net which is strung across the river from bank to bank forming a barrier like a tennis net. Worked into this net are long tubes of netting (pods), which trap the eels and prevent their escape. Just like a tennis net the whole thing can be lowered to the riverbed to allow boats to pass safely over it during the day, but as darkness approaches the eel setter raises the net in anticipation of the creatures coming down on the ebb tide. Those that avoid the eel sett, or other eel men's fyke nets, or the picks and spears of the Breydon wildfowlers, leave the river for the last time and embark on their predestined route westwards. In their final journey they are sustained in the vastness of the ocean by a stream of willow leaf-shaped larvae coming the other way; an inexorable cycle of life, death and re-birth.

Smoked Eel

Smoked eel with a soy sauce glaze is a favourite of the Japanese but, unfortunately for western taste, the main dish is usually preceded by a bowl of clear soup which also contains the eel's stomach. This doubtful delicacy is prized for its health-giving properties, and like all medicines should be swallowed in one gulp. It has been many years since I visited a Japanese restaurant and indulged in this rare treat, and I am yet to be convinced that ingesting something that looked as if it should have been in a jar in the Natural History Museum was in any way conducive to my health, but I've lived to tell the tale! Smoked eel however is indeed a rare delicacy and much prized by our Dutch and German cousins. Prepare them as follows.

Ingredients
Fresh eels
Salt

Method
Live eels are preferable to dead ones but pose the question of how to kill them. The most effective method is to handle the eel with a dry cloth, lay it on a newspaper-covered board (the dry newspaper will help to stop excessive wriggling) and stun it with a sharp blow to the tail. A further blow to the head will ensure that the eel is despatched although muscle movements may continue for some time. Oliver G. Ready, in his description of an Edwardian boyhood in *Life and Sport on the Norfolk Broads,* claims that the only effective way of killing the creatures is to 'get a firm grip of the eel, then throw it with all your force at a brick wall or onto a hard road, so that the whole of its body receives a simultaneous shock, and death', he says, 'will be practically instantaneous.' Hmm, I've never yet had the courage to try it. Complete the process by beheading and splitting the eels, removing the guts and bones, while leaving the skin on. I then usually wrap all the waste up in the newspaper and dispose of it back into the sea where the crabs make short work of recycling everything. Brine as for herring, but leave the eels in the brine for a good two hours. Remove and air dry until a soft, tacky sheen (a pellicule) appears on the skin after 2-3 hours. Rack up in the smoker and cold-smoke over oak shavings for at least 6 hours, double that time for very large specimens. Give them a good blast of heat for

the last half-hour to hot-smoke and partially cook them. Allow to cool, then the skin can easily be removed; leave it on if you intend freezing them. Eat within a week or store in the freezer for not more than 3 months.

Serving

Treat the smoked eels in a similar way to smoked mackerel fillets. Having removed the skin, chop into bite-sized pieces and serve cold with horseradish sauce and salad. Alternatively, fry them gently in butter and serve warm with a squeeze of lemon juice, or follow the Japanese and add a glaze of thickened Soy sauce.

Stewed Eels

'How are we going to cook 'em?' said Bill. 'Stew 'em?' Like his young friends, Bill was a founder member of the Coot Club bird protection society in the second of Arthur Ransome's classic Broadland children's tales *The Big Six*. The question came when the Coot Club paid a nocturnal autumn visit to old Harry Bangate's eel sett up-river from Horning and had been rewarded for their night's labours with half a dozen good-sized eels *(Anguilla anguilla)*. 'There's stewing,' said the old man, 'and souping, and frying and smoking. But you won't try smoking'. Bill and his chums saw this as something of a challenge and ignoring the old eel man's advice decided to smoke them with rather less than successful results. They begged a bagful of shavings from one of the Horning boatyards, but it contained too much pitch pine and cedar, leaving the eels with a decidedly sooty taste. (See the section on smoking for a better method.) Jane Grigson, in this recipe, basically agrees with old Harry but goes further in celebrating the oily richness of the eel in a robust stew with lots of red wine and brandy, which reveals its French origins. They call it *Matelote d'Anguille*, the reference to a mariner acknowledging the eel's curious link with the sea. For as mature adults they forsake their freshwater homes and head for the open ocean to breed far away in the Sargasso Sea of the western Atlantic, and then they die.

Matelote d'Anguille

Ingredients

2 pounds of eel, skinned and cut into chunks
3 tablespoons of brandy
8 prunes
4 tablespoons of oil
Salt
Freshly ground black pepper
One bottle of red wine
Plain flour
Butter
2 cloves of garlic
One large onion, one large leek
Bouquet garni

Eel

107

Method

Spitch-cock the eel (a traditional term of obscure origin allied to 'spatchcock') by slitting the belly, removing the guts and skinning it by cutting round the neck and peeling off the skin like a glove; finally wash the fish thoroughly in salted water. Marinate the eel in the oil and brandy and season well. At the same time steep the prunes in some of the red wine and leave both overnight in the fridge. When you are ready, simmer the rest of the wine with the garlic, onion, leek and bouquet garni for 30 minutes. Put the eel, prunes and liquors in a fireproof shallow pan and pour on the seasoned wine, straining out the vegetables etc.; the eel and prunes should be just covered. Stew gently for 20-30 minutes. Thicken the sauce with the flour and butter, add the garnish and take it to the table in the cooking pan.

Serving

Traditional French garnishes include small glazed onions and button mushrooms sweated in butter served with triangles of fried bread (*Loir*), or the same with bacon and prunes added (*Vouvray*). Serves 8.

Herring Roes: Soft and Hard

The great east coast herring fishery exploited the vast shoals of fish that gather in the autumn on the offshore North Sea banks in their annual migration to the winter spawning grounds in the Sandettie region of the English Channel. Fish caught at this time are known as 'full herring', a term deriving from the fully developed hard or soft roes that the fish contain. Hard roes are the female eggs whilst soft roes, or milt, are produced by the male herring. Herring caught later in the season, 'shot herring' or 'spents', will have shed their roes and are visibly leaner and longer and do not come to the table with anything like the presence of a 'full'. The traditional way of cooking roes, hard, soft or a mixture of both, is simply to roll them in seasoned flour and gently fry them in butter; most gourmets will claim that soft roes are far superior to hard. With a little practice you can tell whether a full herring contains soft or hard roe by gently running your finger and thumb along the fish's flanks. Unlike humans, there is a distinctive difference between the softer male herring's abdomen and the firmer, less yielding female! Another helpful clue is that in longshore herring the females tend to be plumper and bigger than males; this may be the only way that the attendant at the supermarket fish counter (I can't call them fishmongers) will allow you to gender-select your purchases. I reckon to get it right about eight times out of ten. In the local markets on the northern coast of France quite the opposite will hold true. You will be invited, if not expected, to examine the fish on offer and make your selection as part of an almost religious ritual. It is not accidental that Dunkirk's Shrove Tuesday celebrations, before the Lenten fast, take the form of a herring festival, where the local worthies kick off proceedings by chucking herring to the cheering throng from the Town Hall balcony.

The heyday of the Home Fishing was the decade before the Great War, and the following Edwardian recipe comes from that era when it was the custom to serve spicy savoury bites at the very end of a meal. Both Gentleman's Relish and Croque Monsieur, a version of Welsh rarebit, were created for this purpose at this time. The intention was to clear and stimulate the palate of the gentlemen diners before partaking of liqueurs, port and cigars, while the ladies discreetly withdrew to the drawing room. Nowadays, in these less formal and more equality-conscious times, this highly flavoured dish makes a wonderful high tea or supper that can be enjoyed by all diners.

RECIPES FOR FISH ROES AND FISH EGGS

Soft Herring Roes on Toast

Ingredients
4 slices of thick-cut white bread
6 ounces of butter
8-12 pairs of soft herring roes
2 ounces of flour
One level teaspoon of Cayenne pepper
2 level teaspoons salt
Lemon juice
Parsley garnish

Method
Cut the crusts from the bread, toast the slices, spread with butter and place in a pre-heated oven to keep warm. Mix the flour, Cayenne pepper and salt, place in a plastic bag and use this to coat the separated roes thoroughly by carefully shaking so as not to break them. Gently fry them in butter for 1-2 minutes per side. Don't over-cook; they should remain a delicate creamy colour inside when done.

Serving
Place the roes on the toast, sprinkle with lemon juice and garnish with the parsley. Serve nice and hot. As a spicier variation you can use fried bread spread with Gentleman's Relish as a base, topping the roes with a sprinkling of cheese. Finish under the grill. Serves 4.

Use up any leftover roes to make a savoury soft roe butter as described on p. 131.

Hard Roe Taramasalata

In its native Greece taramasalata is traditionally made from the roe of grey mullet, but although grey mullet come inshore to the Norfolk coast in the summer, over many years of catching them I have rarely found one containing roe. The reason is almost certainly that the fish spawn in early spring (one known spawning ground is off the Scilly Isles) but by the time they reach Norfolk their eggs and milts have long been shed, and come the colder weather they migrate back offshore. Use smoked cod or sea bass roe as a highly acceptable substitute; hard herring roe, sadly, will not produce the same result. To smoke your own roe carefully place it in one of those fine mesh net bags the supermarkets use for packaging fruit; salt in the same way as herring and hang alongside the fish in the smokehouse.

Ingredients
4 ounces smoked cod or sea bass roe
Thick slice of white bread (crusts removed)
One clove of garlic
Olive oil
Lemon juice
Black olives or capers

Method
Remove the skin of the roe and soak in cold water for an hour or two. Moisten the bread with a little water and place in the blender. Add a little olive oil and blend, gradually adding the roe and keeping the mixture workable with more olive oil. Finally season with the lemon juice. Refrigerate.

Serving
Serve well chilled in a shallow dish (brown earthenware is traditional) garnished with the black olives or capers. Provide thin toast, or toasted pitta bread.

Sea Trout Roe

In gutting your sea trout you may be lucky enough to find a pair of orangey-red roes. Don't throw them away, use them to make a most acceptable substitute for that highly prized, highly nutritious and highly expensive product of the Caspian Sea, caviare. Salmon or sea trout roe are sold commercially under the name of keta caviar.

Ingredients
Roe of sea trout or salmon
Onion
Lemon juice
Brandy
Salt and pepper
Hard-boiled eggs

Cream cheese
Spring onions

Method
Remove the membrane from the roe and gently break it up into a basin, being careful not to crush the eggs. Chop the onion very finely to a pulp and carefully fold into the roe. Add the brandy and lemon juice, season to taste.

Serving
Serve on small squares of toast and butter, or some good dark rye bread. Accompany with chopped hard-boiled eggs and cream cheese, sprinkled with finely chopped spring onion or chives.

The Icehouse opposite Hall Quay, Great Yarmouth

CHAPTER FOUR
WINTER

Night and day the seas we're daring,
Come wind or come all the winter gales,
Sweating, or cold; growing up, growing old,
As we hunted for the shoals of herring.

The Shoals of Herring - a song of the sea broadcast in 'Singing the
Fishing' August 16th 1960 by Ewan McColl

The Back End

As the back end of the year approaches and the days shorten through
October, winter frosts come with the long nights, and the season's run of cod
starts moving around the coast of East Anglia. They too are searching for the
shoals of herring, or at least for the herring's eggs that coat the sea bed and
provide a rich feast for these hungry scavengers. Norfolk's beach anglers
prepare by sharpening their hooks and oiling their reels, ready for the word
that the cod *(Gadus callarias)* have appeared off Southwold, in the
knowledge that by Christmas they should see some good night-fishing off the
Yarmouth beaches and further north.

The commercial fishermen know the habits of the cod as well, and they
too start to prepare their gear. While deep-sea fishermen favour trawling for
cod, the longshore fishermen use a different method called long-lining.
Packs of coiled lines, often comprising two hundred or more hooks are
baited with pieces of cut herring or whiting; traditionally the fishermen of
Cromer favoured mussels, cracked-open whelks or even oysters. Nowadays
the packs of baited lines are made up when the weather prevents the boats

Long-lining

112

from going to sea and are then stored in the freezer ready for when the boats can get out. The lines are then laid out to sea in a favoured spot as the tide starts to run, a skilled operation that requires great care to avoid being hooked and dragged overboard. Anchored to the seabed and marked with dahn buoys, the lines are left overnight and retrieved at the following slack tide. This method catches only mature, high-quality specimens and under-sized fish can usually be returned live to the sea to grow to maturity. This contrasts with trawling, which tends to catch all sizes of fish, many small and damaged, with the result that the fish command a lower price at market.

Bank Lining

The resourceful residents of coastal villages use an adaptation of the beach fishermen's and the long-liner's methods by laying a bank line to catch cod. This is a many-hooked line, often baited with lugworms *(Arenicola marina)* dug from the very sandbank on which the line is laid. With a heavy lump of lead anchoring the seaward end, the baited line is laid at late low water as far out to sea as the tide permits (this will need to be a spring tide) with the other end tied to a convenient groyne or a stake driven into the beach. The tide slowly covers the line, and with luck the incoming water also brings in the cod as they search for tasty morsels on the sandbank. These may be unwary soft-shelled kittywitches caught in the open, or early lugworms peeking out of their burrows, also greeting the flood tide in anticipation of a meal of minute water creatures.

The bank fisherman waits until high tide has come and gone and then steadily hauls his line to the shore, always ready to grab any poorly hooked fish that may flip into the breakers at the last moment. Cod, flatfish such as plaice or flounders, whiting *(Gadus merlangus)* and sea bass are all caught by this method, a good haul will see a dozen or so fish coming ashore on a spring tide.

In the years following the second world war, a popular method of fishing Norfolk beaches was with a baited long line which, having been carefully laid out in a regular pattern on the beach, was cast out to sea with a short pole made from a broom handle equipped with a small spike in the end. This method predated modestly-priced fibreglass or carbon fibre beach-caster fishing rods, and a skilled operator could cast his line many yards out to sea. Just such an expert was 'Sixer' who fished Eccles beach all his life. Since his school days he had rejoiced in this nickname, applied because he always put six hooks on his bank line.

Cod, Haddock and 'Fish 'n' Chips'

There can be little doubt that the demise of the North Sea cod fishery is upon us, a decline that started back in the 1880s with the success of fleet fishing and, year on year, has threatened us ever since. When I started bank-lining thirty years ago, a ten or twelve-pound fish off the beach was quite common; now it's a real rarity. Cod are officially sized as follows:

Small codling - less than 21½ inches (54cm)
Codling - 21½-25 inches (54-63cm)
Sprag - 25 -30 inches (63-67cm)
Cod – over 30 inches (76cm)

Several of my neighbours and I can tell of catching large cod of twenty-five pounds or more by pulling them by hand out of the shallows; in my case I used a spade as I happened to be digging for lugworms at the time. This act of good fortune stems from the cod's occasional habit of coming in to bask in the sandy shallows, perhaps to rid itself of annoying skin parasites. But these 'fishy' tales are now just memories and even deep-sea trawlers only rarely land large cod of thirty pounds or more.

Cod

Members of the *Gadus* family, cod *(Gadus morhua)*, haddock *(Mellanogramus aeglefinus)*, pollack *(Pollachius pollachius)* coalfish *(Pollachius virens)* or occasionally ling *(Molva molva)* are all used in preparing the ubiquitous fish and chip takeaway, the cornerstone of British fish-eating. The invention of this dish in the 1870s played a defining, and highly nutritious, role in the lives of working class people. Dickens writes of Londoners eating fried fish in *Oliver Twist*, and fried chipped potatoes became popular in Lancashire in the 1860s. We don't know who actually combined the two into the familiar dish that we know today, but we do know that it was instantly popular. Indeed, historians claim that the easy availability of fish and chips from the thousands of chip shops, which soon sprang up in every Edwardian high street, was an essential factor in winning

114

both world wars. The dish provided factory and foundry workers with a hot, tasty and sustaining midday meal to help them meet the demands of wearisome war work. With the essential ingredients coming from the honest toil of both farmer and fisherman, eating fish and chips became almost a patriotic duty on the 'home front', and the Governments of the time recognised the role of the dish as a morale booster by never putting fish and chips on ration.

When peace came and industrial workers went on holiday, their demand for the dish increased rather than diminished. Since many of their seaside holiday destinations such as Fleetwood, Whitby, Great Yarmouth and Lowestoft, also happened to be fishing ports, the availability of really fresh fish ensured that fish and chips became an essential part of the holiday experience. There soon developed distinctive regional variations, Yorkshire folk, for example, demanding chips cooked in beef dripping. This practice is still adopted by Great Yarmouth's Market Place chip stalls in deference to the many northern visitors who continue to make their annual pilgrimage to the town; whilst a distinctive north-south divide between haddock and cod is still apparent across Britain today. Here in East Anglia it is the port of Lowestoft in Suffolk that has taken the leading role in the trawl fishery and their catches mostly supply the fish and chip trade. The port's annual fish festival, held in June, continues to celebrate the importance of fish to the economy, and to the cultural heritage of the town.

This Victorian invention of deep-fried fish in batter changed both the fishing industry and the habits of the nation by introducing the practice of commercial filleting. Up until then fish had been sold whole and the filleting process had been undertaken at home. The art of the fishmonger was born. This enabled large fish markets to dispose of the leftovers and less popular cuts of fish and it has to be said that the all-enveloping coating of batter often concealed some pretty sub-standard fare. These days chip shops know that they simply won't get away with such practices and will ensure that their fish supplier knows it too! Well-prepared fish and chips, using the freshest ingredients and good quality fish, is one of life's great gastronomic experiences, an essential feature of British life, but it is one that may soon disappear.

At the time of writing, fish and chip shops are still able to offer imported cod and haddock in ample quantities at modest, albeit rising prices, but many believe these days are numbered despite, or some say because of, European Union conservation policies. Farmed cod is already a reality, but the fish are prone to the same problems as farmed salmon. Closely penned fish are highly susceptible to disease, and come to the table with a much higher fat-to-lean ratio than wild fish. Current research is looking at ways of ranching fish over much larger areas of water as a means of overcoming these problems. Meanwhile there is no doubt that both cod and haddock thoroughly deserve their popularity. They are wonderfully meaty, tasty, and versatile fish, which deserve better than always being encased in batter, where their true flavours may often be heavily masked by the deep-frying process.

RECIPES

Aunt Ruth's Cod Wrapped in Bacon

The meaty nature of cod is well reflected in this recipe that marries it to bacon, which itself marries wonderfully with tomatoes in all sorts of situations. The result is wonderful, but I wouldn't go quite as far as some who swear that combining simply poached cod with last Sunday's leftover roast beef gravy is the only way a true cod lover should eat the fish!

Ingredients
One pound of inch thick (25mm) cod fillets (or haddock)
4 tomatoes
Tomato paste
Half a pound of streaky and back bacon (try using bacon off-cuts)
A little olive oil
A little butter
Salt and pepper
Clove of garlic (optional)

Method
Cut and trim the cod fillets into four good-sized portions and season each one. Mix the tomato paste and olive oil, brush the mixture all over the fillets. Take a few good rashers of the back bacon and stretch and flatten them. Carefully wrap each fillet in the bacon, putting the streaky on first and finishing with the flattened back bacon to form a neat parcel. Use cocktail sticks to secure the bacon as necessary. Place the fillets in a shallow casserole dish with a little more olive oil. Slice the tomatoes over each fillet; add a few dabs of butter to baste them and the crushed garlic cloves if you are using them. Place in a moderate oven for 15-20 minutes until nicely browned. Remove the fish parcels from the casserole dish and keep warm. Make the gravy over a gentle heat by crushing half the cooked tomato slices into the juices, adding more oil and tomato paste if required to achieve a thin pouring consistency. Give the gravy a final boil and stir to thoroughly deglaze the dish.

Serving
Arrange the fish parcels onto warmed plates and decorate with the remaining tomato slices; pour on the gravy. Serve with sauté potatoes and green beans. Serves 4.

Salt-Baked Cod and Roast Vegetables

This method of baking a whole fish buried in a pile of salt is wonderfully simple, and is also perhaps the recipe that gets the closest to cooking the fish in its natural environment. The salt completely covers the flesh of the fish but barely penetrates the skin; don't be led into thinking that the resultant taste is anything like salt cod, where the fish will have been split, brined and then dried over a long period. The method works well for virtually any whole fish including sea bass, grey mullet or large flatfish. Using the freshest fish is essential to ensure that the salt will capture and entrap all the goodness, giving a wonderfully moist and flavoursome result.

Ingredients
One whole cod (around 2-3 pounds, 1-1.5 kilos) or bass, mullet etc.
3 pounds (1.5 kilos) of coarse salt
Bunch of fresh herbs (fennel, dill, rosemary, lavender - whatever you prefer)
Boiled wild rice
Mixed vegetables suitable for roasting

Method
Gut and clean the fish but do not remove the skin (or scales). If necessary remove the head to ensure that it will just fit, with at least a quarter of an inch gap (6mm.) all round, into your large ovenproof pot. In the meantime pre-heat the oven to a moderately hot temperature (around 220°C). Fill the cavity of the fish with your favourite herbs. Spread a half-inch (12½mm) layer of salt on the base of your pot; place the fish on this layer and then completely bury in the rest of the salt, making sure a good half-inch (12½mm) salt layer covers all. Run your hand under the cold tap and flick a little water over the salt (every Aga owner uses the same technique to freshen up a loaf of bread before popping into a hot oven), this will help the salt to form a sealing crust. Bake the fish for about 30 minutes (allow 10 minutes per pound and another 5 to be sure); remove the pot from the oven and allow it to rest for a few minutes before turning it out onto a large platter.

Serving
Take the fish to the table in its mound of salt, surrounded with a suitable garnish. Break open the crust to reveal the fish underneath. Scrape away the salt and pull off the skin to discover the perfectly cooked and moist flesh in all its succulence. Have a 'bone plate' handy to take all the spent salt and rubbish. Accompany with boiled wild rice and a platter of roasted mixed vegetables (peppers, shallots, sugar snap peas, baby corn etc.) drizzled with olive oil and baked in the same oven.

Wylaway Fisherman's Pie

Wylaway is a simple timber and cladding bungalow, tucked neatly in the lee of the dunes just a few yards from the shore, in one of those hidden parts of the Norfolk coast which only local knowledge will reveal. Over many years, summer and winter, the family holidays and long weekends of the owners have been whiled away at

Wylaway as a respite from their busy city lives. Being so close to the beach means that sea fishing and shrimping have always formed an essential part of the vacation, and with luck provided the major ingredients for this tasty dish. With the view inland from Wylaway being over fields planted with good Norfolk main-crop potatoes, we should not be surprised that this fisherman's pie has evolved as a firm family favourite.

Ingredients

These may vary according to the catch of the day or available leftovers, but the basis of the dish should always be one of the firm white-fleshed fish that flake nicely into bite-sized chunks. Flat fish are usually considered too soft and delicate for this dish, but the addition of a few chunks of salmon or sea trout will never go amiss, adding richness and variety.

One pound of whitefish (cod, whiting, haddock, sea bass, grey mullet, rock salmon)
Half pound of salmon or sea trout (optional)
4 ounces of shelled shrimps or prawns
4 ounces of cockles, mussels or chopped whelks (optional)
4 ounces of dressed crab or lobster meat (optional)
Third of a pint of milk
One bay leaf
2 large onions
2 pounds of potatoes (mashed)
6 ounces of grated cheese
Flour
Butter
Salt & pepper

Prawn

Method

Gut, scale and fillet the fish. Season with salt and pepper. Place in a deep ovenproof dish with the finely chopped onion and bay leaf; cover with the milk and poach gently for 20 minutes. In the meantime boil and prepare the mashed potatoes. Remove the fish from the liquid and place to one side; thicken the stock over a low heat with the flour and butter and remove the bay leaf. Flake the fish removing all remaining bones and return to the thickened stock together with the remainder of the shellfish. Stir in the mashed potatoes and most of the cheese; adjust the seasoning. Brush the top with a little milk and sprinkle over the rest of the cheese. Bake in a hot oven or place under the grill for a further 10 minutes.

Serving

Serve as a fancy starter in washed-out crab or scallop shells with mashed potato piped round the edge. For a main course serve with braised winter root vegetables. Serves 6.

Seafood Pancakes made with Whiting

A slender and smaller relative of the cod, whiting *(Merlangus merlangus)* are silvery fish with a greeny/golden sheen. They shoal along the Norfolk coast in late autumn and early winter, preceding their larger cousins by several weeks. A tasty, albeit quite bony fish, whiting won't keep their fine watery flavour very long so they make an ideal basis for this popular dish. The basic mixture is much the same as fisherman's pie, made a little richer by the addition of eggs, dry white wine and single cream, and aided by the meltingly tender flesh of the fish, which gives the mixture a velvety texture. Prepare the fish by beheading, gutting and cutting out the backbone to leave a triangular fillet. The fish can also be smoked like this, both Finnan Haddie and Arbroath Smokies may be made from split whiting as well as the usual haddock. A mixture of smoked and unsmoked whiting makes this dish even more interesting.

Ingredients
One pound of whiting fillets
Half pound of cooked salmon or sea trout (optional)
4 ounces of shelled shrimps or prawns
4 ounces of cockles, mussels or chopped whelks (optional)
4 ounces of dressed crab or lobster meat (optional)
Third of a pint of milk
Cup of white wine
One bay leaf
2 large onions
Flour
Butter
3 hard-boiled eggs
Single cream
Grated cheese
Pancake batter to make 8 pancakes

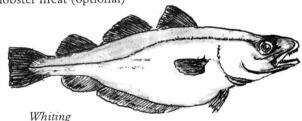

Whiting

Method
Make the pancakes in the usual way with a batter made from egg, flour and milk, but keep them slightly thinner than you would on Shrove Tuesday so that they fold more easily. Stack carefully and allow to cool. Make the filling as for the fisherman's pie but reserve some of the thickened stock. Add the fish and chopped boiled eggs to the remainder and heat gently, finally using single cream to stiffen the mixture. Place a couple of spoonfuls of the filling in a line down the middle of each pancake and carefully roll them up. Place in a shallow dish and pour on the reserved stock. Sprinkle with the cheese and place in a hot oven or under the grill for 5 minutes.

Serving
Serve with a simple chopped parsley garnish, swimming in the white sauce, crusty bread to mop up the sauce and the rest of the bottle of dry white wine. These pancakes are wonderfully rich and shouldn't be hurried so another bottle in reserve is recommended. Serves 8 starters or 4 main courses.

The Sprat Fishery

The winter cod of course are following a rich source of food that comes inshore to join the herring in the near-shore waters of the Norfolk coast at this time. As the New Year dawns the east coast longshoremen turn their attention to the great shoals of sprat *(Spratus spratus)* which appear as if from nowhere. These small silver slivers shoal in vast quantities, so dense that as they move through the water the propellers of fishing boats often churn the fish into a watery soup, greedily relished by the following gulls.

Sprats are caught using fine-meshed nets in a similar way to the herring; in a good year the herring will also last through February and March and the longshoreman will cast a fleet of nets of different mesh sizes to catch both species. Herring usually feed on plankton but, in several reported cases of mistaken identity, claims for herring containing live young have been made. Whilst such biological aberrations cannot absolutely be discounted, the explanation is usually that the herring has eaten a sprat and the remains have subsequently been discovered. Young herring look very similar to sprats; the best way to tell the difference is to run your thumb along the sprat's belly towards the tail where you can easily detect the saw-toothed scales which form a sharp keel; the herring's underside is quite smooth. Very young herring and sprat fry are often found swimming together; when caught, battered and deep fried they appear on the plate as whitebait. Many of us eat sprats without knowing it, for that couple of tins of Norwegian brisling (called sardines) lurking in the kitchen cupboard are none other than brined and lightly smoked sprats canned in oil. In the nineteenth century, sprat banquets were popular all along the east coast, and the Southwold sprat fair was an important annual event intended to celebrate this bounty of the sea.

Smoked Sprats

Sprats are smoked in a similar way to bloaters by lightly brining the ungutted fish (about 40 minutes in the brine will do) and then spearing them through the gill onto pointed lengths of stout wire and hanging them for around 3-4 hours in the smokehouse. Half a dozen smoked sprats make a fine starter when served with warm bread and butter. Remove the head and tease out the small amount of guts, skin them if you prefer. Lightly grill (if skinned add a scant dab of butter) and serve with a simple salad and lemon quarters; for a sharper taste, dress with one of the fruit vinegars.

Fried or 'Tempura' Battered Sprats

Sprats can be treated in a similar way to herring by rolling in seasoned flour and frying in butter, or deep-frying in oil. Alternatively make up a simple 'tempura'

120

batter by whisking plain flour with sparkling water and adding a little salt. Coat the fish in batter and deep fry in hot oil at 365°F (185°C). Tip the smoking hot fish into a large communal pot and serve immediately (they definitely won't wait) with lemon wedges and bread and butter. Fingers are by far the best way of eating fried sprats, simply twist and pull off the head, at the same time teasing out and discarding the gut and backbone. Eat the rest, tail and all. Use the same technique to produce what the Italians call *Fritto Misto*, a variety of deep-fried strips of fish pieces *(goujons)* which may also include prawns, squid or scallops. Serve with one of the savoury butters described in Chapter 5.

Salt Sprats

If you enjoy a tin of brisling, you will certainly enjoy this dish, which gives a superior treatment to the humble sprat, turning it into a gourmet treat.

Ingredients
Fresh sprats
Coarse cooking salt
White wine dressing (see p. 128)

Method
Behead and gut the sprats, wash thoroughly and then dry in a tea towel. Place a half inch layer of salt in a casserole dish, add a layer of sprats, then another layer of salt, sprats and so on. Put in the fridge overnight. In the morning remove from the salt, dust off and cover with the white wine dressing, store in the fridge until you are ready to serve.

Serving
Serve as an hors d'oeuvre with thin pieces of melba toast.

Whelks, ancient and modern

Both whelks *(Buccinum undatum)* and winkles *(Littorina littorea)* belong to the group of shellfish called gastropods (the name means 'stomach foot'). Unlike cockles, which are bivalves with two shells, gastropods have only one shell, which as often as not is twisted into a spiral. They usually twist in a clockwise direction, but you can occasionally find contrary specimens with an anti-clockwise spiral. In geological circles Norfolk is famous for a fossil whelk called *Neptunea contraria*, which is found in rocks laid down during the last Ice Age, (the sands and gravels of the river bank at Bramerton just outside Norwich are a typical locality); its shell is always twisted anti-clockwise. Scientists believe that this genetic aberration may have resulted from the intense cold of the period. Traditionally the whelk season commenced in Norfolk towards the end of autumn when, with the onset of winter (nothing like the winter of an ice-age), crabs retreat to their holes for their winter hibernation. At this time the Cromer crab boats would often temporarily re-locate to more sheltered, sandier beaches such as Mundesley or Bacton for the better launching conditions that they provide in the stormy winter weather, and to be closer to the whelk grounds. As well as being caught for food, whelks were used as bait for long lines. Whelks are caught offshore using specially made pots, which are baited and secured to the seabed in much the same way as crab or lobster pots. A traditional whelk pot was made from a heavy iron frame, bound with tarred rope to form a cauldron-shaped pot, but these days tough white plastic buckets with a fringe of netting are used. These are weighted down with a layer of concrete placed in the bottom. I wonder whether in a hundred years time they will start to appear in antique shops in the same way as the old iron pots do today?

Whelks are marine snails, and treating them in the same way as the French treat Roman land snails *(Helix pomatia)* will provide a fine meal. They can also be included in an *Assiette de Mer*, but for both dishes they will first need to be boiled. In this country whelks have had a bad press in the past few years (not that the fishermen care since most of the British catch finds a ready market on the Continent), and a badly cooked whelk can indeed be tasteless and rubbery rather than a subtle cross between chicken and lobster, which is how they should taste. Shop-bought whelks will have been boiled in salted water, but both the flavour and texture of the creature can be greatly enhanced by the court bouillon technique which follows. This method will also prove successful in cooking the whelk's smaller gastropod cousin, the winkle.

Boiled Whelks (and Winkles)

Ingredients
Fresh whelks - preferably alive
One onion
One carrot
Cup of white wine
Bay leaf
Peppercorns
Brine - 3 tablespoons of salt per pint of water

Winkles

Method
Give the whelks (winkles) a thorough scrub under running water and place them in a large cooking pot, ensuring that they are well covered with the brine. Add the other ingredients and bring to the boil, simmering for about 10 minutes. Allow to cool, discarding the court bouillon.

122

Using a fork (a pin for winkles) flick off the platy operculum at the opening of the shell and with a twisting motion remove the meat. The last part of the meat to emerge, 'the trail', is quite edible but less firm than the rest, and some people prefer to discard this section. Add to an *Assiette de Mer*, or serve with a mayonnaise dip (see Chapter 5) and bread and butter.

Whelks in Garlic Butter

Whelks are merely the garden snails of the sea and one of the best treatments is to do exactly what the French do with their Roman snails and turn them into a flavour-packed, and calorie-packed starter.

Ingredients
Boiled whelks
Two cloves of garlic
Butter
White wine
Salt and pepper
Chopped parsley
Grated cheese (optional)

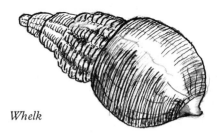

Whelk

Method
Chop the boiled whelks into small cubes that will easily fit back into the scrubbed-out shells. Finely chop the garlic and fry in the butter; add the wine and bring to a good bubbling boil, then add the whelk meat. Simmer for a couple of minutes; add the chopped parsley and then spoon the mixture (which should be moderately stiff) into the mouth of the shells.

Serving
Place in a warmed casserole dish and pour on a little more melted butter to glaze the shells; if you wish sprinkle with a little grated cheese. If you have used shop-bought whelks without shells, serve in small ramekins. Keep hot in the oven or under a grill until ready, serve on one of those dimpled white ceramic dishes which are to be found in every French hypermarket or up-market kitchen shops in this country, with French bread and a white wine.

A Word about Pawkin' and Seaweed

While winter storms put an end to fishing, they also bring other bounty, for when the north-east wind blows on the Norfolk coast (we call it a 'lazy ol' wind'; it goes straight through you rather than going around!) it has the effect of scouring the seabed and tearing bottom-living creatures from their normal resting place. These will include starfish *(family Asteriidae)* and sea anemones *(phylum Coelenterata)*, lumps of coal from long-sunk freighters, seaweed and sometimes nuggets of amber, the 'gold of the north' the Vikings called it. All of this debris gets tumbled together and cast up onto the shore-line for beachcombers, both avian and human, to paw through in search of useful trifles; I've even seen a fox working the strand line after a storm. In times past, beachcombing ('pawkin' in Norfolk dialect) was an important source of income for longshoremen, and the collection of seaweed for fertiliser was but one commercially-inspired winter activity. Most species of seaweed cast up on the beach are edible. Some are more edible than others, but clever cooks can always find ways of using whatever nature sends their way to produce a tasty dish. You may rarely discover **Sea Lettuce** *(Ulva lactuca)* on a Norfolk beach, which is perhaps the most palatable seaweed you will find. As the name suggests, it is bright green, broad-leafed and fairly tasty, but it lacks the crispness of garden lettuce. Look for it especially where a stream of fresh water flows out to sea. Serve raw with a twist of lemon as an accompaniment to other seafood. **Bladderwrack** *(Fucus fusiculosis)* has long, black, or dark brown fronds which are pimpled with bubbles of air that enable them to float close to the surface and gain the light they need to survive; at the other end the plant has a tough swollen base which anchors it to the rocks or pebbles of the seabed. **Serrated Wrack** *(Fucus serratus)* is similar in appearance but the fronds are flatter with a toothed edge and a much lighter greeny-buff, colour. Neither of these species is really edible but they are the ones usually used as a base for an *Assiette de Mer*, and also in this next recipe where they impart that distinctive 'essence of the sea' to both the fish, and the sauce you serve with it.

Grey Gurnard Steamed Over Seaweed

Grey gurnard *(Eutrigla gurnardus)* are little known and somewhat underrated white fish, frequently used as bait for crab pots, for their commercial success is limited by the high head-to-body ratio, which produces much wastage. An inshore shallow-water fish, I sometimes find them in crab pots, especially if the pots have been left for a while due to bad weather. As bottom-living creatures they are usually caught by trawling, and in times past the crew would often be given any gurnard the ship caught as a perk at the end of the voyage, to sell on the market as 'stockie bait'. The gurnard (in Norfolk dialect they are called 'latchets', which may have something to do with the fact that the live fish emits a distinctive grunt when handled) has an enormous head and a tapering spotted body with distinctive pectoral fins. The first three rays of the fin are feeler-like spines and the main part is splayed like a bird's wing. Strange-looking it may be, but the close flesh makes good eating; it smokes well and is often simply baked, but this recipe adds that extra ozone-packed punch to make it even better. You don't have to use gurnard; the recipe will work well for most white or flatfish.

Ingredients
6 fillets of grey gurnard (about one and a half pounds)
One and a half pounds of bladderwrack
Half a pint of fish stock (See Chapter Five)
Dab of butter

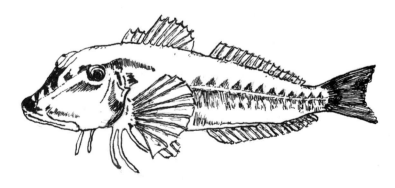

Bladder wrack

Method
Blanch the seaweed by adding to boiling water for one minute, remove and drain in a colander, rinsing it well under a cold running tap. Place the seaweed in a wide pan large enough to take the fillets in a single layer and pour on the fish stock. Bring to the boil and immediately turn down the heat to a gently steaming simmer. Carefully lay the fish on the top of the seaweed and put on the lid; the aim is to steam the gurnard not poach it. Depending on their thickness, the fillets should be cooked in around 6 minutes, remove from the pan onto a warmed plate and keep warm. Strain the stock into a shallow pan and reduce by rapid boiling; whisk in the butter.

Serving
Simply serve the fillets on a warm platter surrounded with some of the seaweed and suitably garnished with parsley, lemon slices etc. Pour on the sauce and take to the table. Serves 6.

Gurnard

CHAPTER FIVE
MARINADES, FISH STOCK, FISH SOUP
COURT BOUILLON, DRESSINGS, BUTTERS AND SAUCES

'**Marinade** sb : [Fr marinade, Sp marinada, It marinare]
to pickle in brine; from French marine.'
Oxford English Dictionary

Marinades and dressings

Marinades are all about steeping the fish in a seasoned liquid to flavour or tenderise the creature. Indeed, marinating the delicate flesh of fish may often be the only process needed to actually 'cook' it and make it palatable. This process is often referred to as *caveach* (or *seviche, cebiche* or even *escabeche)*, words which have their origins in the Mediterranean countries of Spain and Portugal. Given the ready availability of citrus fruits in these countries, the active ingredient of any marinade, that which actually alters and sets the protein of the flesh to a distinctive opaqueness, will be a fruit acid such as lemon or lime juice. In this country chefs have discovered that the acetic acid contained in malt or fruit vinegars acts in a similar way. All these ingredients modify the flavour of the fish, and over the years any number of combinations of fruit juices, spices, herbs and seasonings have been devised to enhance the flavour and texture of the raw material. The high acid content of these marinades can also suppress the growth of moulds and fungi and act as a short-term preservative for the fish in dishes such as soused herring. Once the marinade has done its initial job it may be used as a basting liquid to retain moistness when grilling, or as a basis for a sauce to further complement the flavour of the fish.

Olive Oil and Lemon Juice

This is the simplest form of fish marinade and dressing. Combine the two ingredients in the proportion five parts of olive oil to one part of lemon (or lime) juice. Steep the whole fish or fillets in this mixture prior to barbecuing or grilling, then use it to keep basting the fish when on the grill. As a dressing, drizzle the mixture directly onto the fish, or serve the fish with lemon wedges and a decanter of oil to allow diners to mix it to their own taste. From a good delicatessen you may be able to purchase bottles of Lime or Lemon Olive Oil, in which the olives have been pressed together with the fruit, producing a powerful intrinsic blend of juice, zest and oil.

Orange and Green Peppercorn Marinade

A light and refreshing marinade, suitable for a 2-3 pound whole fish, mullet, bass or even oily fish such as mackerel. This is also a good dish for the barbecue but double-wrap the fish in foil if using this method.

Ingredients
2-3 pounds of mullet, bass or mackerel
One red onion
2 small oranges
6 tablespoons olive oil
2 tablespoons cider vinegar
One tablespoon of lightly crushed peppercorns
Chopped fresh parsley to garnish
Salt

Method
Gut and clean the fish, slash both sides with 3-4 diagonal cuts. Line an ovenproof dish with sufficient foil to parcel the fish. Slice the onions and oranges, lay half in the bottom of the dish, put in the fish and cover with the remaining slices. Pour on the remainder of the ingredients, season and allow to marinade in the fridge for a good four hours. Baste occasionally. When ready to cook, pre-heat the oven, loosely wrap up the fish parcel and bake in a moderate oven for 15 minutes per pound plus 15 minutes.

Crab or Lobster Oil

This is yet another way of extracting the flavour from the debris of crustaceans to make a salad oil dressing for serving with just about any fish or shellfish dish you care to name.

Ingredients
Lobster or crab shells
Grape-seed oil

Method
Put the shells into a shallow heatproof dish, pouring over sufficient grape-seed oil and a couple of tablespoons of water, just enough to cover them. Put to the heat and bring gently to the boil, then transfer to a low oven to simmer for about 30 minutes. Remove from the oven and allow to cool thoroughly. Strain into a jar and store for up to a month in the fridge. Grape-seed oil is a fairly light, flavourless oil that readily takes up flavours from other things without masking them.

Serving
Use as a salad dressing or lightly drizzle directly onto fish or shellfish dishes.

Lime and Ginger Marinade

This marinade is especially good for sea trout or salmon, the ginger giving a clue to its oriental pedigree. (See p. 78 for a Japanese Soy sauce) Slice the raw fish as thinly as possible (you will find it easier to do this if you put the fillet in the freezer for a short time). Refrigerate the slices until you are ready to add the marinade just prior to serving.

Ingredients
4 fluid ounces of groundnut oil
Quarter of an ounce of fresh ginger (finely chopped)
One teaspoon of pink peppercorns
One lime
Pinch of salt

Method
Make the dressing by simply combining all the ingredients.

White Wine Dressing

Ingredients
4 teaspoons of olive oil
4 teaspoons of groundnut oil
4 teaspoons of dry white wine
One teaspoon of white wine vinegar
Pinch of salt

Method
Simply mix the ingredients and use as a salad dressing.

Fish stock

The purpose of making fish stock is to extract all the goodness from the parts of the fish which are too tough to eat, and use the resultant fragrant broth to enhance the flavour of those parts which you do want to eat. The best fish stock comes from fish such as turbot or sole, which contain a lot of gelatine, but virtually any white fish trimmings from cod, bass or whiting will produce a fine result. Avoid using oily fish such as herring or mackerel. In these days of commercial food preparation you can buy good quality fish stock cubes that are a perfectly acceptable alternative to the home-made product, while in French supermarkets you will find any number of special regional fish stock powders marketed under the general name of *Fumet de Poisson*. Use as a basis for fish soups, bisques, sauces and that paragon of Mediterranean fish cookery, the bouillabaisse.

Ingredients

2 pounds of whitefish debris: heads, skin, fins and bones
One large carrot
One onion
Cup of white wine
One celery stick
One sprig of thyme
One bay leaf
Fresh parsley
Pepper and salt
Water

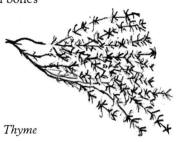

Thyme

Method

Place all the ingredients into a large pan (break up the bones if necessary) and bring to the boil. Reduce the heat (overheating will produce a fish glue!) and simmer for no more than 30 minutes, thus ensuring that the stock will not turn bitter. Don't be tempted to liquidise the debris for this will also impart bitterness to the stock. Skim off the scum during the simmering then strain and allow to cool to a jelly before using.

Usage

Stock makes an excellent basis for fish stews and soups. You can also reduce the stock by boiling off in a wide pan as a basis for a sauce. When reduced it will thicken and turn syrupy. Any leftover stock may be frozen as ice cubes for future use.

Fish Soup

Fish soup should contain a mixture of different sorts of fish to obtain the best flavour and texture. In meat cookery it is the cheap cuts of meat that make the most flavoursome soups, chiefly because they contain more gristle than the leaner cuts, and the same holds true for fish. Cheaper whitefish such as whiting, cod, gurnard or mullet are ideal, but you should also include one of the cartilaginous fishes such as dogfish or skate, for the 'gristle' in these species will give essential body to the soup. Oily fish such as mackerel or herring are not suitable for souping.

Ingredients

2-3 pounds of fish
6 ounces of onion roughly chopped
6 ounces of celery roughly chopped
6 ounces of leek roughly chopped
6 ounces fennel roughly chopped
6 cloves of garlic, peeled and roughly chopped
Grated lemon peel
4 large tomatoes
Tomato paste
Small red pepper (remove the skin)

One bay leaf
Large pinch of saffron
Large pinch of cayenne pepper
Salt and pepper
5 fluid ounces of olive oil
3 pints of water

Method

Fillet the fish and use the heads, bones, skin etc. to make a fish stock as described in the previous recipe. Heat the olive oil in a large deep pan and add the onion, leek, celery, fennel and garlic. Sweat for about 30 minutes until the vegetables are soft and slightly browned, then add the lemon peel, tomatoes, tomato paste, pepper, bay leaf, saffron and the fish fillets. Turn up the heat and fold everything together until thoroughly mixed, then add the stock. Bring to the boil and simmer for about 40 minutes. Liquidise the soup; strain it by rubbing gently through a sieve and return to the pan and reheat it. Taste and adjust the seasoning with salt, pepper and the cayenne to give it a distinctive bite.

Serving

Serve in warmed bowls with garlic croutons or crostino (See p. 36) dusted with grated parmesan.

Court Bouillon

This is a flavoured cooking liquid used to poach fish or shellfish to ensure that the flavour of the fish is not lost in the cooking liquid. When it comes to poaching fish, using plain water for this purpose will only serve to extract all the flavour from the flesh leaving a tasteless specimen, which is fine if you want to make a fish soup, but not so good if you intend to eat the fish itself. Plain water poaching causes desirable fishy flavours, contained in complex chemicals and essential oils, to be lost through the cell walls of the fish by a process called osmosis. In order to prevent osmosis occurring during the poaching process, the cooking liquid must be of a higher concentration than the liquids in the cells of the fish meat. The answer is to make a court bouillon. The idea is also to add vegetable flavours to the flesh of the fish as part of the cooking process. By using the court bouillon you extract the natural essences of the vegetables, thus preventing osmosis occurring, and cook the fish to a tasty succulence.

Ingredients

One carrot
One onion
One stick of celery
Half a cup of white wine
One bay leaf
2 sprigs of thyme
Black pepper (ground or whole corns)

Salt
2 pints of water

Method
Place all the ingredients in a pan and slowly bring to the boil; simmer for 30 minutes. Strain and allow to cool. Substitute different herbs such as fennel or dill for variations depending on the fish you intend poaching. Use this as a poaching liquid for any whitefish or shellfish, ensuring that the fish is completely covered by the stock and is gently brought to the simmer from cold.

Savoury Butters

Used mainly as a lubricant with fried or grilled fish, savoury butters are made by combining herbs or sauces with softened butter and rolling the mixture in greaseproof paper to form a cylindrical block. This is then well chilled in the fridge, which makes it easier to cut into slices for serving at the very last minute as an accompaniment to the dish. Use fresh herbs whenever possible for best flavours and choose salted or unsalted butter according to your taste. Savoury butters can be prepared well in advance (often using up leftovers) and kept in the freezer until required; slice straight from frozen using a warmed knife or cheese wire.

Soft Roe Butter

Poach the soft herring roes in lightly salted water for three minutes; alternatively give them one to two minutes on medium power in the microwave. Allow to cool and then pound the roes into 4 ounces of butter and add a teaspoonful of lemon juice. Taste and adjust the seasoning.

Maitre d'hotel Butter

Fold a teaspoonful of finely chopped fresh parsley with 4 ounces of soft butter and a teaspoonful of lemon juice. Taste and adjust the seasoning.

Horseradish Butter

Cream 2 teaspoonfuls of finely grated horseradish with a quarter pound of butter and a pinch of paprika.

Lobster Butter

Pound the coral from a hen lobster (usually about 2 ounces) with a quarter of a pound of butter, a sprinkling of mace, a pinch of cayenne (to intensify the colour) and 2 teaspoons of lemon juice. This butter can also form the basis of a lobster sauce (see below).

131

Basic and Specialist Fish Sauces

Sauces are made from a rich combination of ingredients and comprise the basic elements of marinades and court bouillon; essentially their active ingredient derives from the flesh and bones of the fish itself (but not the innards) in the form of a basic fish stock. Stock is essential for making sauces, the active ingredient in this process being the natural gelatine found in the fish, especially in the head. This raises the concentration of the liquid and, by complex chemistry, locks in all the goodness. In this way you can extract flavours and essential oils from the parts that you don't want to eat, i.e. the head and fins, and then use these to make a sauce to accompany the part you do want to eat. Spices, herbs and seasonings also enhance sauces and they are used as an accompaniment to the taste of the fish rather than as a modification to its original flavour. Sauces usually rely on the addition of fats and oils, such as cream and butter, to the stock to enhance the flavour and provide smoothness. The addition of flour or cornflour also modifies the texture and thickens the stock to give a pouring sauce that acts as a lubricant. There are five basic sauces commonly used to accompany fish, and countless variations of these sauces in which herbs, stock, spices and parts of the fish, such as roe, tomalley or the natural juices from shellfish (i.e. oysters), are added to the basic sauces to make interesting flavours and textures. Largely based on classical French cookery, the basic sauces are White sauce, Béchamel sauce, Velouté sauce, Hollandaise sauce and Mayonnaise.

White Sauce

The simplest of sauces made by quickly combining butter and flour (a roux) in equal quantities in a pan put to a moderate heat, and then gradually adding sufficient milk to achieve the desired consistency stirring all the time. Simmer gently for a couple of minutes more, finally adjusting the seasoning with salt and pepper.

Béchamel Sauce

This sauce uses the same ingredients and method as white sauce with the addition of strained fish stock to replace, partially or completely, the milk to give a more flavoursome result.

Velouté Sauce

In this case the butter and flour mixture (roux) is cooked in the pan for a little longer to achieve a light brown colour and only then is the liquid (fish stock, milk)

132

gradually added. Velouté sauce is usually made richer with the addition of a little cream, and given even more colour by adding an egg yolk. Thinned with more fish stock this sauce makes a good soup, completed with the addition of cooked shellfish meat, or it may be further thickened and added to puff pastry vol-au-vent cases as an hors d'oeuvres.

Hollandaise Sauce

This is a highly-flavoured sauce which combines the butter typical of a sauce and the acids and spices typically found in marinades. The technique relies on forming an emulsion where the fat droplets of the butter are suspended in the liquid ingredients, a process that requires some care to prevent the two separating (curdling).

Ingredients
2 tablespoons of wine vinegar
4 crushed peppercorns
3 egg yolks
6 ounces of butter
A few drops of lemon juice
Half a cup of water
Salt and pepper

Equipment
A double boiler (bain marie)

Method
Boil the vinegar, peppercorns and water in a pan to reduce the volume by one third. Strain into the top pan of a double boiler, which is on a slow simmer, and whisk in the egg yolks over this gentle heat until thickening begins. Add the butter, either melted or in small pellets to retain the heat of the mixture and prevent curdling. Add the lemon juice; taste and adjust the seasoning. Keep warm in the double boiler until ready to serve.

Mayonnaise

Mayonnaise is one of the most important fish sauces in its own right without the addition of further flavourings. Use it as an accompaniment to fried, grilled or barbecued fish and shellfish, either on the side of the plate or by providing a medley of raw vegetables as dipping sticks to aid in the transfer of the sauce from the bowl. 'Mayo' forms the basis of the ubiquitous Tartare Sauce which, even when served in plastic sachets, still holds poll position among the sauces provided in seafood restaurants across the land. Indeed 'mayo' itself may also be found similarly confined and perhaps just as tasteless, but good quality ready-made mayonnaise is universally available for home consumption in modern supermarkets. The taste of superior 'mayo' derives from good quality olive oil and fresh raw eggs, so if you have access to a few free-range hens to supply the latter it's well worth making your own.

If not, stick to the shop-bought stuff, if only for the reassurance that the contents of the jar will be devoid of the salmonella bug. This bacterium, with which even the best kept hens and their eggs may be infected, does nothing to harm the hens but can affect 'at risk' humans. This recipe uses lemon as a base flavouring but may be simply adapted to any of the other citrus fruits or herb-based flavourings such as tarragon or rosemary; spices such as mustard and saffron produce colourful and tasty results. The addition of a dollop of tomato paste and a few drops of Tabasco will of course produce the pink Sauce Marie Rose accompaniment to prawns and shrimps, but does nothing to explain something which has always puzzled me; why, I wonder, is prawn cocktail always served in a cheap wine glass? Finally, aioli is a garlic-based mayonnaise traditionally used with salted fish.

Lemon Mayonnaise Dip

Ingredients
2 egg yolks
2 teaspoons white wine vinegar (never be tempted to use malt vinegar)
A small cup-sized jug of best olive oil (or a 50:50 mixture of olive and sunflower oil)
Pinch of salt
Lemon juice

Method
Ensure that all the ingredients have been allowed to reach room temperature before you begin. Whisk the egg yolks in a bowl with the lemon juice, white wine vinegar and salt (place the bowl on a damp teacloth for security as you won't have a hand free to hold it). Slowly drip the olive oil from the jug into the bowl, whisking continuously at a steady, measured pace until you have added the same amount of oil as the rest of the ingredients. Having achieved a stable emulsion you can now add the rest of the oil at a faster pace, but you must keep whisking, whisking, whisking. When all the oil is used up, taste the result, adjust the seasoning, adding more salt or lemon juice as necessary. If it curdles you can save the day by putting another egg yolk in a clean bowl and whisking in the curdled stuff, again drop by drop.

Mustard Mayonnaise

Add 2 teaspoons of Norfolk mustard powder to a few drops of water and add to the bowl with the other ingredients prior to adding the oil.

Saffron Mayonnaise

Use the same basic technique as above with a couple of pinches of saffron strands, but in this case use hot water to draw out the colour of the saffron.

Tarragon/Rosemary Mayonnaise

Roughly chop the herbs to produce 2-3 teaspoons, place in the bowl and scarcely cover with boiling water. Leave for a couple of minutes to cool, then drain and proceed as above.

Aioli

Blitz 6 cloves of garlic in a food processor; add the other 'mayo' ingredients and blitz again, finally adding the olive oil bit by bit, blending the mixture for 10 seconds each time.

Creamed Horseradish Sauce

Although you can buy commercially prepared, creamed horseradish, making it yourself not only ensures freshness but also allows you to adjust the strength of the condiment to your own taste. Horseradish sauce is traditionally eaten with roast beef, but when made with single or pouring cream this milder and lighter creamy sauce is a perfect accompaniment to grilled fish. The heavier sauce is also an essential ingredient of smoked mackerel or kipper pâté. Horseradish *(Nasturtium armoracia)* grows well by the sea and favours sandy soil; indeed in my garden it is a persistent weed, but at least the light soil makes it is easy to dig up!

Ingredients
3-inch (8cm) piece of fresh horseradish root
One tablespoon lemon juice
2 teaspoons of sugar
Half a teaspoon of English mustard powder
Half a pint of double cream

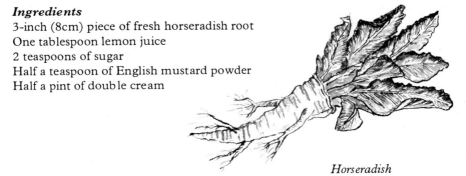

Horseradish

Method
Having given the root a good scrub, peel it and then grate it finely or place in a food processor. Take care, young fresh horseradish root can be violently pungent and more than one incautious cook has had to evacuate the kitchen with streaming eyes when the lid of the food processor has been removed. Mix the grated horseradish, lemon juice, sugar and mustard in a bowl. Whip the cream until it stands in soft peaks, gently fold into the horseradish mixture. Refrigerate and use within 2 or 3 days.

Creamed Mustard and Dill Sauce

When Jeremiah Colman started milling mustard in the 1840s at Stoke Holy Cross, just outside Norwich, he produced a home-grown spice which perfectly complemented the hot dishes of the Indian sub-continent that were popularised by returning members of the British Raj; mustard became all the rage. This sauce combines the hotness of English mustard with the Scandinavian subtlety of the aniseed flavour of dill, offset by a hint of sweetness, and all set in a creamy sauce. Use it as an accompaniment to grilled flatfish dishes such as sole, plaice, dab or flounder. The old adage that Jeremiah made his considerable fortune not from the mustard people ate, but from what they left on the side of the plate, will not hold true in the case of this deliciously spicy sauce.

Ingredients

One ounce of butter
One and a half tablespoons of plain flour
Fish stock (made from trimmings)
One tablespoon of white wine vinegar
3 tablespoons of chopped fresh dill
One tablespoon of English mustard
2 tablespoons of caster sugar
2 egg yolks
Salt and pepper

Dill

Method

Melt the butter and stir in the flour; cook for 1-2 minutes over a low heat. Remove from the heat; gradually stir in the stock then return to the heat, bring to a low boil and simmer for 2-3 minutes. Remove from the heat, beat in the vinegar, dill, mustard and sugar. Beat the egg yolks in a small bowl and very slowly add to the pan, whisking all the time over a very low heat to prevent curdling.

Serving

Provide ample bread to mop up the sauce.

Gooseberry Sauce

One pound of gooseberries
2 ounces of butter
2 tablespoons of sugar
Pinch of ground mace
Salt

Gently simmer the topped and tailed gooseberries with a little water for about 20 minutes until soft. Liquidise the pulp or rub through a sieve. Melt the butter in a pan and add the pulp, sugar, nutmeg and salt. Beat well and taste to adjust the seasoning, adding more mace or salt to get a good sharp flavour.

136

Asparagus Sauce

Ingredients
10 ounces of asparagus spears
2-3 tablespoons of single cream
Cupful of fish stock
Salt and pepper

Wash the asparagus carefully under cold water, break off any tough ends where the stalk will snap easily and cut the stalks obliquely into 2-inch (5cm) lengths. Simmer the stalks in the stock until tender. Remove the more tender tips after 4 minutes and keep to one side; give the remainder a couple of minutes extra. Drain and reserve the cooking liquid. Put the stalks into a food processor and reduce to a brilliant green purée. Thin the purée to a good sauce with the reserved liquid, adding a spoonful or two of single cream to achieve a pouring consistency. Taste and adjust the seasoning, refrigerate until ready for warming and serve with the reserved tips.

Samphire Sauce

Using the same asparagus sauce recipe you can substitute boiled samphire ('poor man's asparagus') to make the greenest of green sauces. Simply remove the woody parts, boil for 10 minutes, strip off the flesh and then reduce in a food processor with butter or single cream. Season with pepper but never, ever, add more salt.

Lobster Sauce

Ingredients
Tomalley and/or the coral of the lobster
Fish stock
2 egg yolks
2 ounces unsalted butter
Lemon juice
Pinch of cayenne pepper

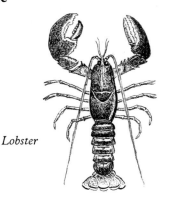

Lobster

Equipment
A small metal mixing bowl
A large saucepan into which the bowl will fit

Method
Bring a couple of inches (5cm) of water to the boil in the large saucepan. Place the egg yolks and a little fish stock into the mixing bowl and whisk over the boiling water. Both the coral and tomalley are protein which, when heated gently, will thicken the sauce, but too much heat will cause them to coagulate. Beat in the tomalley and/or coral and continue beating until the sauce begins to thicken.

Remove from the heat and whisk in the butter, piece by piece. Add a little lemon juice and a pinch of cayenne.

Mushroom Sauce

You can use ordinary shop-bought mushrooms for this dish, but, even better, try picking some wild field mushrooms. As summer turns into autumn and the morning mists start to settle on the meadows, these normally underground members of the plant kingdom are stirred into producing their above-ground fruiting bodies with a flavour which will always outstrip any commercially raised fare. If you can find a good source of other woodland mushrooms such as ceps or chanterelles then their flavours and textures will add an extra dimension to this sauce. If the nearest autumn meadow happens to be too far away don't despair, for the better super-markets will often offer such varieties.

Ingredients
One ounce of butter, cubed
Half a tablespoon of oil
One small onion finely chopped
Quarter pound of mushrooms (roughly chop the largest)
Quarter pint of reduced fish stock
One tablespoon of fresh chopped chervil
Half a tablespoon of fresh chopped parsley
Salt and pepper

Method
Heat half the butter with the oil and fry the onion until tender. Raise the heat and put in the mushrooms, stirring occasionally until they are cooked through. Add the fish stock, chervil, parsley, salt and pepper and bring to the boil, simmering for 2-3 minutes (longer if your fish stock has not been previously reduced). When the mixture has turned syrupy, reduce the heat and whisk in the rest of the butter to thicken the sauce. Taste and adjust the seasoning.

Serving
Serve piping hot (either just made or zapped from frozen in the microwave) with any white fish such as brill or turbot. Eat immediately; neither the sauce nor the fish will stand delay.

Rosemary

138

Glossary of Fishing Terms

Allis Shad	*Alosa alosa* – a large member of the herring family
Anadromous	Fish which spawn in fresh water but mature in the sea
Bank Line	A beach long line fitted with multiple hooks laid at low tide
Baulk	A slender stick fitted with hooks on which herring are hung for kippering
Bloater	A herring salted and lightly smoked without being gutted
Beatster	A person (usually female) who repairs a herring net
Braider	One who makes (braids) a trawl net
Broadster	A female crab or lobster
Buckling	A hot-smoked and thus partially cooked herring
Butt	The Norfolk word for a flounder
Cart	The Norfolk word for the detached shell of an edible crab
Catadromous	Fish which spawn in the sea but mature in fresh water
Crinny	The net tunnel by which crabs enter the crab pot
Dahn	A flagged buoy used to mark the location of an anchor, pot, net etc.
Dab	A small flat fish *(Limanda limanda)*
Dan Leno	A short weighted stick used to keep a net from folding
Deaf Ears	The Norfolk phrase for the gills of an edible crab
Dead Men's Fingers	The gills of an edible crab
Drift Net	See Herring Net
Double-ender	A traditional east coast beach fishing boat, pointed at both ends.
Ebb Tide	The outgoing tide
Elver	An immature eel
Fathom	A measure of sea depth, rope or netting equivalent to six feet
Fleet	A train of herring nets joined together
Flood Tide	The incoming tide
Fyke Net	A long tube of netting and hoops used to catch eels in various river locations
Gill Net	See herring net
Gipping	A method of removing the long gut of a herring through the gills prior to pickling.
Herring Net	A net hung vertically in the water in which the fish become entrapped by their gills
Horse Mackerel	see Scad
Kill	A smokehouse (derived from 'kiln')
Kipper	A herring split down its backbone, salted and smoked
Kittywitch	A Norfolk name for a small swimming shore crab
Latchet	A red or grey gurnard
Long-line	A line of hooks coiled into a pack
Loves	Racks fitted into a smoke chamber

Lows	Shallow pools left on the beach when the tide retreats
Maizy herring	Herring running with spawn
Milt	The soft male roe of a herring
Music	The slotted metal base of a crab pot which resembles a musical stave
Neap Tides	Shorter range tides occurring in the first and third quarter of the lunar cycle
Over for the Lord	An invocation for Divine help in securing a good catch (said when casting the first net overboard)
Pawkin'	The Norfolk word for beachcombing
Pick	The process of removing crab or lobster meat from their shells
Pod	Part of an eel sett, a long net tube designed to trap the eels
Prick-on	Placing split herring on a baulk for kippering
Ransacker	A man who checks through nets for making repairs
Red Herring or Reds	Heavily smoked and salted herring
Roker	Another word for a skate (*Raja clavata*).
Rouse	Mixing (rousing) whole fish with rough salt prior to smoking
Sand Dab	Another name for the dab (*Limanda limanda*)
Scad	The fish *Trachurus trachurus*, also known as the horse mackerel
Scotch Cure	A method of preserving herring in a mixture of salt and their own oil
Scudding	A term for shaking herring out of the nets
Seine Net	A net with a weighted bottom line used from the shore
Sett	A permanent netting device for catching eels
Sewin	The Welsh name for sea trout (*Salmo trutto*)
Shad	See 'Allis' and 'Twaite'
Shank	A string of crab pots
Sheer	Clear and transparent sea
Shekel	The internal shell of an edible crab
Shimmer	A net full of herring shimmering in the moonlight
Shot herring	See Spents
Skiff	A modern east coast beach fishing boat, usually flat-bottomed of fibreglass construction
Slips	Small Dover soles
Slack water	When the tidal flow slows to a standstill for a few minutes
Speet	A slender stick (spit) on which herring are threaded through the gill for bloatering or wind drying
Spents	Herring which have shed their spawn (see shot herring)
Spring Tides	The longer range tides occurring after full and new moon
Tangle Net	A net anchored to the seabed in which fish become entangled
Thick	When the sea is clouded by disturbed sediment (the opposite of sheer)

Tissot	The rope which takes the strain between the boat and the fleet of nets
Toggs	Undersized edible crabs
Tows	Ropes joining crab pots together to form a shank
Twaite Shad	*Alosa fallax* a large member of the herring family
Wind Drying	A method of preserving fish by drying in cold weather

Glossary of Cookery Terms

Bain marie	A double boiler used to impart a consistent gentle heat to the upper pan
Beurre Manière	A ball of butter and flour used to thicken sauces (see also roux)
Barb	An obsolete term for carving a lobster
Chine	'To chine' is to remove the backbone of a fish (usually salmon)
Caveach	A method of cooking without heat, which relies on acid fruit juices to set the protein
Marinade	A liquid used to flavour fish or meat
Pick	Removing the flesh from the shell of a crab or lobster
Roux	Equal quantities of butter and flour combined as a basis for sauces
Spitchcock	To prepare an eel for the table (now obsolete)
Tame	An obsolete term for carving a crab

Hauling the boat up the beach at Cromer

Bibliography

Bagenal, T.B. (1972)   *The Observer's Book of Sea Fishes*
Frederick Warne

Butcher, David (1980)   *The Trawlermen*
Tops'l books

Faunthorpe, B.R. (1952)   *Shore Fishing for Lobsters, Crabs and Prawns*
Seeley Service & Co Ltd

Forsyth, W.S. (1939)   *Inshore Sea Fishing*
Adam and Charles Black

Grigson, Jane (1973)   *Fish Cookery*
Penguin Books

Grigson, Sophie & Black, Wm. (1998)   *Fish*
Headline Book Publishing

Hodgson, W.C. (1957)   *The Herring and Its Fishery*
Routledge & Kegan Paul

McDonald, Kendal (1980)   *Food from the Seashore*
Pelham Books London

Norwak, Mary (1982)   *Nature in Norfolk - a Heritage in Trust*
Jarrolds

Ransome, Arthur (1940)   *The Big Six*
Jonathan Cape

Ready, Oliver G. (1910)   *Life and Sport on the Norfolk Broads*
T. Werner Laurie

Rundell, Maria Eliza (1805)   *A New System of Domestic Cookery*
John Murray

Schott, Ben (2003)   *Schott's Food & Drink Miscellany*
Bloomsbury

Stannard, David (2002)   *Broader Norfolk*
Larks Press

Stein, Rick (1988)   *English Seafood Cookery*
Penguin Books

Walton, Prof. John K. (2004)   *The Seafood Magazine: The Way We Were - Fish & Chips*
Sea Fish Industry Authority

Weight			Volume	
Ounces	**Grams**		**Imperial**	**mls**
¼	7		¼ tsp.	1.25
½	14		½ tsp.	2.5
¾	21		1 level tsp.	5.0
1	28		½ tbsp.	7.5
2	57		1 level tbsp.	15
3	85		1 fl. oz	30
4 or ¼ lb	114		2 fl. oz	60
5	142		4 fl. oz	120
6	170		¼ pint	142
7	199		½ pint	284
8 or ½ lb	227		¾ pint	426
9	255		1 pint	568
10	284		1 ¼ pints	710
12 or ¾ lb	341		1 ½ pints	852
16 or 1 lb	454		1 ¾ pints	1 litre
2 ¼ lb	1kg		2 pints	1.3 litres

Oven Temperature

Description	°C	°F	Gas Mark	Aga
very slow	110	225		
	120	250	½	very cool
	140	275	1	
	150	300	2	cool
slow	160-70	325	3	
moderate	180	350	4	warm
	190	375	5	medium
moderate hot	200	400	6	medium high
	220	425	7	
hot	230	450	8	high
very hot	240-60	475	9	very high

Index of Fish